A History of
Passenger
Aircraft

A History of
Passenger
Aircraft
William Sweetman

Hamlyn

London·New York·Sydney·Toronto

Acknowledgements

The publishers are grateful to the following individuals and organisations for the illustrations in this book:

Aeroplane Monthly; Aerospatiale; Air France; Airbus Industrie; American Airlines; Gordon Bain; The Boeing Company; Breguet-Aviation; British Aerospace; British Airways; Austin J. Brown; Charles E. Brown; Central Press Photos Ltd.; de Havilland Aircraft of Canada; *Flight International*; Fokker-VFW International B.V.; General Dynamics Corp.; The Hamlyn Group Library; J. Hughes; Keystone Press Agency; Helmø Larsen; Howard Levy; Lockheed Aircraft Corp.; Lufthansa; J. Hughes; McDonnell Douglas Corp.; Novosti Press Agency; North American Space Agency; North American Aviation; Pan American Airways; S. Piercey; The Press Association; Richard T. Riding; Rolls-Royce (1971) Ltd.; Saudia Airways; Brian M. Service; Nigel Snowdon; Chris Sorensen; Sport & General Press Agency; Swissair; John W. R. Taylor; Anton Wettstein.

This edition published in 1979 by
The Hamlyn Publishing Group Limited
London . New York . Sydney . Toronto
Astronaut House, Feltham, Middlesex,
England

ISBN 0 600 37248 0

Printed in Italy by
Group Poligrafici Calderara, Bologna

Contents

Introduction

The illustrious William B Stout, designer of the Ford Tri-Motor, succinctly defined a commercial aircraft as "a vehicle capable of supporting itself aerodynamically and economically at the same time." That definition remains as valid today as it was in the 1920s, when the Tri-Motor was designed. Rigorously applied, however, it would exclude from this volume many of the aircraft which appear in the following pages. It is therefore convenient to relax the definition and to assume that the intention to produce such an aircraft was there, even though many types are included which never made a profit, either for their operators or for their constructors.

Commercial pressure has been the main driving force behind the development of the airliner from the earliest days. Sometimes, military technology has helped: the first heavier-than-air passenger aircraft were derived from the Handley Page and Farman bombers of the First World War, while the Boeing 707 of 30 years later emerged from a long line of German and American military research. The flow of technology has, however, often gone the other way: the all-metal, stressed-skin airliners of the 1930s could outrun the fastest bombers of their day and were entirely the product of civilian research, while the bypass jet (or turbofan) was an airliner powerplant before it became standard for military aircraft.

The history of the airliner is also the story of how Europe, which possessed a commanding lead in aviation in 1919, lost that lead to the United States of America by 1934 and has subsequently spent a vast amount of effort and money on generally unsuccessful attempts to reduce that American lead. To put the scale of US dominance in its proper perspective, three individual types of American jet airliner – the 707, 727 and DC-9 – had each outsold Europe's entire production of jet airliners by 1979.

The main reason for the American success has probably been the isolationism and anti-competitive attitude of the European industry. Until the mid-1950s, the European manufacturers – with the creditable exceptions of Fokker and Junkers – behaved as though their sole function was to supply their own national airlines. The very low break-even production runs of pre-Second World War airliners (often built in batches of less than a dozen) may have made this approach practicable; the advent of stressed-skin construction and the appearance of large and complex airliners in the early 1930s, however, sent the development costs of the average airliner soaring. Such expense could only be recouped over a large production run and the selling of an airliner became almost more important than its design.

After the Second World War, only the British aircraft industry was able to tackle the American manufacturers. In 1946, however, a BOAC order for Constellations started a futile and irrelevent debate over the national airline's alleged duty to buy British, a dispute which was to cloud British aviation policy for the next 30 years. When a British manufacturer decided to build an aircraft that appeared right from the technical and marketing standpoint, it was often successful despite the indifference of the national airlines: examples included the Viscount, the Avro 748 and the BAC One-Eleven. When, on the other hand, a British manufacturer's relationship with the state airlines blinded them to developments in the outside world, the results included commercial failures like the Vanguard, the VC10 and the Trident.

The Trident story was particularly unfortunate. In the late 1950s, the design of the Trident and that of the Boeing 727 were proceeding in parallel; both were about the same size, although with different layouts. In Britain, de Havilland then scaled down the Trident to meet BEA's requirements, while Boeing adopted the Trident layout for their much larger 727. In both 1977 and 1978, the Boeing design comfortably outsold the entire Trident production run.

As a complete contrast to the atmosphere in Europe, consider the climate which produced that all-time classic, the Douglas DC-3 in America. The DC-3 story began with the earlier Boeing 247, which was advanced for its time, but not so advanced that it opened an unassailable lead over the Europeans. TWA, prevented from buying 247s in time to compete with United, approached Douglas for something bigger and better – the DC-2. American Airlines, the third major US transcontinental carrier, then asked for a sleeper version of the DC-2 in order to get one step ahead of both their rivals. Douglas were desperately trying to meet delivery schedules on the DC-2; they were in the early stages of production, notoriously the most unprofitable phase in the history of any airliner. Nevertheless, they knew that a refusal of the American request would simply drive that airline elsewhere, so they proceeded to develop the DC-2 into the DC-3, by which time not even Boeing could afford the time and money to catch up.

Free competition among the airlines and manufacturers in the USA has always been matched by similar

rivalry between the engine builders. Wright and Pratt & Whitney fought a 30-year battle of the horsepowers: when the two manufacturers were competing to power the DC-1, for example, they worked side-by-side in cordoned-off enclosures at the Douglas plant, and the line between them was uncrossable. When a Douglas engineer reported to his superior that the Wright engine was to be chosen, the latter said: "Don't tell them – we may get a good engine out of this contest yet." Eventually, most civilian DC-3s and all the military C-47s had Pratt & Whitney engines. By 1955, it was Wright who held an apparently unassailable lead; yet that company never sold a single commercial turbine engine.

Perhaps the finest example of competition at work, however, was the titanic battle between the Lockheed 49 Constellation and the Douglas DC-4. As soon as one manufacturer proposed an improvement on their aircraft, their rivals would reply with something better. The ultimate developments of both families, the intercontinental DC-7C and the Starliner, were nearly twice as heavy as their forbears.

A book of this size cannot possibly attempt to be a work or reference. Rather, it is a narrative history which aims to illustrate the trends and patterns of an industry which grew from nothing to global importance in less than a normal human lifespan. The story is one of changing fortunes – such as the resurgence of Boeing in the late 1950s and the disappearance of Wright – and of some dead ends, like the passenger airship, the flying boats and the numerous super-giant aircraft that cast their shadows over the industry from time to time. Above all, it is a story of commercial and engineering inspiration and perspiration.

The de Havilland (later Hawker Siddeley) Trident was one of the fastest airliners of its day, but its smaller size and longer runway requirement than the rival 727 kept it out of world markets

The fledgling industry

Sir George Cayley, the most fertile aviation mind of his day, summed up the potential of air transport in the phrase: "The air is an uninterrupted, navigable ocean which comes to the threshold of every man's door." Implicit in this was the idea that aerial navigation could some day be exploited for commercial purposes, in the way in which the British had made seafaring the means to build their global power.

It was obvious that the balloon, the only aerial device to have demonstrated sustained flight in Sir George's time, had no commercial potential beyond pleasure flying. Unlike a ship, a balloon could not make way by opposing the force of the wind to the resistance of the water; it was imprisoned in the air, and went exactly where the wind went. A surprising number of pioneers failed to realise that fitting sails to a balloon would make no difference at all.

Cayley was not one of these, and in 1816 he produced a design for what was to be the first commercial, passenger-carrying air vehicle: the "rigid", steerable balloon, with a number of gasbags contained in a lightweight, internally-braced tubular, covered framework.

This type of craft could not be called a true "dirigible" until it was equipped with an engine of sufficient power to permit it to make headway against a normal wind. The 1800s were a time of experimentation, as various pioneers worked to design an airship which could accomplish this feat.

The problems of the airship designers in their search for a suitable powerplant for their craft were minor compared with those of the determined few pioneers of the heavier-than-air machine. Clement Ader achieved powered flight in the 1880s; Otto Lilienthal eventually lost his life in pursuit of stability and control. By the end of the century many people seriously doubted whether the aeroplane would ever contrive to lift its pilot from the ground, let alone a commercial payload.

The airship was less demanding in terms of the power-to-weight ratio required of its engine, and was easier to control than the aeroplane, so it was not surprising that it matured earlier. Giffard's steam-powered craft of 1852 and the electrically driven *La France* of Renard and Krebs, flown in 1884, were milestones on the way to a practical machine. These airships were non-rigid, single-cell types, unlike the commercial airship projected by Count Ferdinand von Zeppelin in a paper published in 1874. The first Zeppelin flew in July 1900, a 420 ft craft, 399,000 cubic feet in volume, powered by two Daimler petrol engines. Further aircraft of the type followed, and in November 1909 Zeppelin formed what is believed to have been the first company to engage in the commercial transport of passengers by air. DELAG (Deutsche Luftschiffsfahrt AG) started operations in June 1910, and had a maximum fleet of five, 20-seater Zeppelins on their domestic air routes in Germany. By July 1914, DELAG had made nearly 1,600 successful passenger flights.

While Zeppelin built and operated his airships, the development of a safe, stable and reliable aeroplane continued. The Wright brothers are generally accepted as having been the first to achieve stable and controlled powered flight, in December 1903, but their main achievement was the considerable further development which they put into their aircraft between 1903 and 1909. By that time enthusiasts in many countries were developing experimental aircraft, and their number continued to increase in the 1910–12 period. Military evaluation of the aeroplane, mainly for reconnaissance purposes, began in 1908 and by the outbreak of the First World War in 1914, most developed countries had small forces of aircraft in service.

However, two significant developments had taken place in 1913. One was the inauguration of the world's first commercial aeroplane service, using a tiny three-seat Benoist flying-boat. Pioneer Tony Jannus used the aircraft to link the towns of Tampa and St Petersburg in Florida, but the service was abandoned as unprofitable after only a few months. 1913 also saw the first flight of what was then the largest aircraft in the world, and one of the first with an enclosed cabin. Popularly known as *Le Grand*, the aircraft had been designed by Igor Sikorsky and constructed by the Russo-Baltic Carriage Works, a railway-engineering company. Spanning 92 ft, *Le Grand* was powered by four engines mounted between the wings. An unusual feature was the open promenade deck upon which passengers could take the air in flight. *Le Grand* never went into service, but was the forerunner of the Imperial Russian Navy's war-time fleet of 70 Ilya Mouroumets four-engined bombers.

Another large aircraft of pre-war origin was the Porte-Curtiss America, designed for a transatlantic record flight. On the outbreak of war, the America became the prototype for a series of Curtiss patrol boats and their British equivalents.

The 1914–18 war was predominantly a land war, and experimentation with aircraft and aero-engines was not unduly limited by demands for mass-production. The war years thus saw a great deal of technical

progress, particularly in the development of powerful and reliable aero-engines and in the payload-range and handling qualities of large aircraft.

The first long-range bombing raids were made by the German Navy's airships, of the Zeppelin and Schutte-Lanz rigid types. During the war, the quest for height and bomb-load led to airships of four times the volume of DELAG's biggest pre-war craft, equipped with radio navigation aids. When the Zeppelins proved vulnerable to fighter interception, however, it was decided to use aeroplanes for long-range bombing.

top
The world's first four-engined plane, *Russki Vityaz*

above
A charming period study of sophisticated travel in 1919, with passengers embarking from their tiny car into a Sablatnig P111 of Lloyd Luftverkehr Sablatnig Airlines

opposite
The Zeppelin LZ 13 *Hansa* flew with DELAG until taken over by the German Army Corps in 1914. Power was supplied by three 150 hp Maybach engines and it had a cruising speed of 50 mph

Germany's bombers were of two classes: the G type, mostly built by Gotha or Friedrichshafen, and the vast R type (Riesenflugzeuge, or giant aircraft), some of which spanned nearly 140 ft and had four or five engines. The Zeppelin-Staaken works was responsible for many of the R-class, and many advanced designs were in preparation at the Armistice. Britain, meanwhile, had put the Handley Page 0/400 into production, and this large twin-engined bomber was to be followed into service by the four-engined V/1500, designed to attack Berlin, and by the Vickers Vimy. All these heavy bombers were powered by liquid-cooled engines developed shortly before and during the war. The rotary engine used in many Allied fighters was clearly unsuitable for such large aircraft, with its powerful gyroscopic effects.

Most of the in-line wartime engines were built with individual steel cylinders and lightweight sheet-metal water jackets; later in-line engines were manufactured with cast and machined blocks.

The static, air-cooled radial engine, with the cylinders disposed equally around the crankshaft, had not been developed to really high outputs before 1918, but that year saw the Cosmos Engineering Company in Britain developing their nine-cylinder Jupiter radial. The development costs of the new engine overstrained the finances of Cosmos in 1920, and they were taken over by the Bristol Aeroplane Company. The Bristol Jupiter radial went on to become one of the most successful aero-engines of the 1920s.

Two other classic engines had their origins in the USA in 1923–24. The wartime Liberty engine, designed and built by the motor industry, was never extensively used for civil work, and the US Navy preferred radials to the more complex liquid-cooled Liberty. In 1923, the Wright company took over a small firm called the Lawrance Aero Engine Corporation, who were working on a small nine-cylinder radial engine. That engine became the first Wright Whirlwind. In 1924, the Pratt & Whitney company entered the aero-engine business with the first Wasp, starting a competition which was to last more than 30 years. The 500 hp Hornet and Cyclone followed these engines; eventually, Wright dominated the market for piston engines, but the company never made the transition to gas-turbine engines in the late 1950s, and Pratt & Whitney finally won the day. However, there is no doubt that the close commercial competition between the two US manufacturers yielded better engines for the airlines time and again.

In the years immediately after the First World War, however, there was no market for such new engines, because the airline industry was slowly becoming established with the aid of the many cheap, war-surplus aircraft. In Europe, the lead had been taken by the aircraft manufacturers, who saw the de-

velopment of air transport as a way of filling their suddenly empty post-war order-books. Among the first companies to start operations was DELAG, who resumed their Friedrichshafen-Berlin airship service with the new LZ-120 *Bodensee*, with 30 seats. However, both this and a sister ship were confiscated by the Allies as potential weapons of war.

The same fate befell the advanced Staaken E.4/20 airliner, a high-wing cantilever monoplane with an enclosed cabin for 18 passengers and four 245 hp Maybach engines. The structure was of aluminium alloy, and the wing was built as a single massive box-spar, like that of a modern airliner. The E.4/20 was flown in 1920, but the Inter-Allied Control Commission, worried about the military potential of the aircraft, ordered that it should be scrapped. They may also have been worried by

the commercial competition such an aircraft would present. The Staaken aircraft bore a remarkable resemblance to the British Armstrong Whitworth Atalanta, developed ten years later.

Some of the smaller types developed by Professor Hugo Junkers, whose theories were extensively used in the design of the E.4/20, escaped the Allies' vengeful eyes. In June 1919, Junkers flew the first F.13, a small low-wing, single-engine monoplane transport that adopted the all-metal construction and characteristic Junkers corrugated-alloy skin of the wartime J.10 ground-attack type. The F.13 could seat four passengers in an enclosed cabin, and no fewer than 322 of the type were built between 1922 and 1932. Some of the first F.13s were operated by the Junkers company's own airline subsidiary, and these later went into

Trimotors old and new: American Airlines arranged this meeting to mark the introduction of the first US three-engined transport (the Boeing 727) since the Ford Tri-Motor. Both aircraft are owned by American, the Ford carrying 13 passengers at 100 mph, the 727 taking almost 100 passengers at around 600 mph

top
One of the first new aircraft produced after the First World War was the Junkers F13. This all-metal monoplane had an enclosed cabin for four passengers

above
The De Havilland D.H.16 was a cabin version of the wartime D.H.9, an open cockpit two-seat aircraft built in vast numbers. Subsequently used by civil operators for a variety of purposes, the cabin conversion accommodated four passengers

tain height after an engine failure, so a failure even in a multi-engined type meant a forced landing. Landing speeds were low, however, and with a skilled pilot a forced landing could often be accomplished without injury to passengers or major damage to the airframe.

The other classic among early airliners was also a product of German wartime development, in this case the last of the highly successful line of fighters designed by the Dutchman Anthony Fokker. The D.VIII monoplane carried its wing on struts above the fuselage. The wing was built of wood, and covered with plywood rather than fabric, permitting a deep, stiff cantilever structure without bracing struts or wires. The same basic wing design was to characterise Fokker designs right through the 1920s and 1930s.

The first Fokker transport was the single-engined, four-seat F.II, operated by the newly formed Royal Dutch Airlines (KLM). It was followed by the more powerful five-seater F.III, with a single 360 hp Rolls-Royce Condor. About 1923, Fokker moved his company back to his native Holland, setting up his factory near Amsterdam. His first two transport designs introduced the fabric-covered, steel-tube fuselage that was to be Fokker's other hallmark.

The British and French manufacturers, meanwhile, had gone into air transport with adaptations of their wartime aircraft. The Aircraft Manufacturing Company, or Airco, started airline operations in mid-1919, as soon as wartime restrictions were lifted. Air Transport & Travel, as the airline was known, were formed to operate Airco-manufactured aircraft designed by Geoffrey de Havilland and known by their creator's initials. AT&T started operations with a few D.H.4As, converted from D.H.4 day bombers by the addition of a simple wooden "lid" over the aft cockpit; and D.H.16s, developed from the D.H.9A and seating four passengers in an enclosed cabin. However, AT & T were forced out of business by competition from subsidised foreign carriers in late 1920. The

service with Deutsche Lufthansa when the state airline was formed from a merger of many small carriers in 1926. F.13s were flown as landplanes and floatplanes, and were powered by Junkers, Mercedes and BMW in-line engines.

The use of a single engine on a passenger aircraft may seem strange to modern minds, but in the early days of air transport the safety of an aircraft in the event of an engine failure depended on the ability of the pilot and the aeroplane ·to make a safe engine-out forced landing. It was to be some time before even a three-engined aircraft could main-

British Government's reaction was to provide a subsidy for British airlines, but Airco (later de Havilland) did not resume airline operations. Instead they sold their new airliner designs, the D.H.18 and the similarly sized but much improved D.H.34, to new carriers such as Instone Air Lines and Daimler Air Transport. The D.H.34 was a ten-seater biplane with a crew of two, powered by a single Napier Lion engine developing 450 hp. (The Lion was liquid-cooled with 12 cylinders arranged in three banks of four, and was highly successful in airline service until the Jupiter was developed.) As operated by Daimler – complete with uniformed steward – the D.H.34 could carry a spare engine in the baggage compartment to rescue another stranded en route.

In August 1920, the British Air Ministry sponsored a competition for a large airliner. Vickers produced a civil version of their Vimy bomber, which had entered service too late for the war but had made headlines with the first-ever non-stop heavier-than-air transatlantic flight in the previous year; Bristol converted the incomplete third prototype of their Braemar triplane bomber into the 14-seat Pullman, but the competition was won by the 15-seat Handley Page W.8. The new airliner was the world's first large commercial aeroplane. Although it bore a family resemblance to the 0/400 and its 0/17 commercial development, with which Handley Page Air Transport had started operations, the W/8 was an entirely new design. The W/8 and its descendants, including a three-engined version called the Hampstead, served with Handley Page and later with Imperial Airways until 1931. Some of the type were built by SABCA in Belgium for that country's national airline, Sabena.

Several wartime French manufacturers collaborated to set up the Compagnie des Messagéries Aériennes (CMA) after the war, this airline becoming Air Union in 1923 and Air France in the 1930s, following the absorption of smaller airlines. Bleriot, Breguet, Caudron and Farman were among the

founders of CMA, and in their early days the airline was largely equipped with single-engined Bleriot Spad biplanes, seating four to six passengers. The Bleriot biplanes remained in production in successively improved versions, until 1930.

The biggest type used in the first years of Air Union operations, however, was the Farman F.60 Goliath. More than 60 of these 12-passenger twin-engine biplanes were built, and from 1921 they were put into service on CMA's main routes to London, Brussels and Berlin. Like many airlines at the time, CMA operated an extremely large variety of differ-

top
Many First World War D.H.4 two-seat bombers were converted for civil use. The D.H.4A was a conversion which housed two passengers, facing each other in a glazed cabin behind the pilot's open cockpit

above
The Handley Page W8 was the company's first pure civil transport aircraft. Built of wood and fabric, it carried 15 passengers in adequate comfort at a cruising speed of 90 mph

right, top and opposite
The incredible pace of development in civil aviation can be seen by comparing the Vanguard of 1928 with the technology of fifty years later, when shirtsleeved British Airways pilots could fly effortlessly almost anywhere in the world in wide-bodied jets like the Lockheed TriStar

centre, upper
A production Handley Page W9 in Imperial Airways livery and powered by three 420 hp Bristol Jupiter VI engines

centre, lower
Like so many of the very early airliners, this Breguet 14 was converted from a bomber variant for use by Messageries Aériennes of Paris

bottom
The sole Vickers Type 170 Vanguard was developed from the Vickers Victoria troop-carrier which served with the RAF for a decade. Imperial Airways used this 22-passenger aircraft for route-proving trials in 1928

ent types and variants, and the Goliaths were eventually powered by a range of engines including May-bachs, Renaults, Armstrong Siddeley Jaguars and Bristol Jupiters. The Goliath was an advanced aircraft for its time, with a weatherproof enclosed cabin, and remained in service until 1933. Another Farman type was the strange-looking Jabiru, with an unusual long-chord monoplane wing. Versions of the Jabiru were built with two, three and four engines.

In 1924, the British Government decided to amalgamate the country's airlines into a new company, known as Imperial Airways, and it was envisaged that this airline would set up air routes throughout the Empire. The Daimler, Handley

Page and Instone companies were all merged into the new operator, which soon established a record as a safe and competent, if highly conservative airline.

One of Imperial Airways' first decisions was that future aircraft built to their specifications should all be multi-engined; in their first year, they ordered new types from Handley Page, Armstrong Whitworth and de Havilland. First to arrive were the Handley Page W/10s, Lion-powered developments of the W/8; they were followed by the Armstrong Whitworth Argosy, with three Jaguar radials, built as 28-seaters for the airline's European services. With steel wing and fuselage structures, the Argosies proved highly durable, and remained in service until 1935. The third new

type was the de Havilland D.H.66 Hercules, designed specifically for the hot weather and high airfield elevations of the long, eastbound route to Australia, blazed by Sir Alan Cobham in a series of proving flights shortly after Imperial Airways were formed. Although it was more powerful than the Argosy, with three 420 hp Jupiters, the Hercules carried only seven passengers in addition to its load of mail.

As Imperial Airways and KLM extended their routes eastward, Lignes Aeriennes Latécoère pioneered the French South Atlantic mail services with a series of Latécoère-designed single-engined mailplanes. The Atlantic crossing itself was made by surface vessels until the mid-1930s, but Latécoère (later Aeropostale) pioneered services from France to Senegal, and from Natal in Brazil over much of South America.

Germany's pioneering was largely carried out by the flying-boats of the Dornier Wal series. The first of these all-metal monoplanes, with their

above
Le Bourget airfield in 1921, with a pair of Potez 9s on hand

left
The Armstrong Whitworth Argosy was powered originally by three 385 hp Armstrong Siddeley Jaguar III engines. The type was used exclusively by Imperial Airways and only seven were built

opposite, top
Designed from the outset as a bomber, the Farman F 60 Goliath became an important civil transport produced in many variants

opposite, centre
The Handley Page W10 was flown on most of Imperial Airways' regular routes during the late 1920s. Powered by two 450 hp Napier Lion engines, the W10 accommodated 16 passengers

opposite, bottom
The three-engine D.H.66 Hercules was noted for its reliability. Originally used on the Cairo-Karachi route by Imperial Airways, West Australian Airways purchased four for use on their Perth-Adelaide service

characteristic broad hulls, sponsons and twin tandem engines, was built in 1922 in Italy to frustrate the occupying powers, who had ordered an earlier Dornier craft sunk in 1920. The basic design, much improved and enlarged, remained in production until 1933 and the same general arrangement was adopted for the Do18. Developments included the four-engined Super-Wal, which entered service with Lufthansa in 1928.

Imperial Airways introduced flying-boats for the Mediterranean sectors of their Eastern routes in 1929. The chosen type was the first of many flying-boats built for Imperial Airways by Shorts of Rochester, the three-engined Calcutta biplane. Of all-metal construction, apart from fabric covering

top
A small number of Dornier Do R Super Wals were built during the latter half of the 1920s. This was a larger, twin-engined version of the Wald powered initially by Rolls-Royce Condor water-cooled engines arranged in tandem. In addition to the crew, the Super Wal carried 19 passengers

centre
The Fokker F.XII was one of a long line of Fokker trimotors. Originally ordered by KLM, the type also flew with Swedish, British and Danish airlines. Power for this 16-passenger aircraft was supplied by three 425 hp Pratt & Whitney Wasp C engines

bottom
Providing some small measure of refinement for the pilots as well as for their passengers, this Short Kent (*Satyrus*) was used by Imperial Airways in 1931. The enclosed cockpit featured sliding roof panels

on the wings, the Calcutta carried 15 passengers and was powered by Jupiters. At the same time, the Italian carriers SISA, SAM and later Ala Littoria were extending their Mediterranean services. One of the most unusual types used by the Italian carriers was the Savoia Marchetti S.55, a monoplane flying-boat with twin hulls and tandem engines carried above the centre-section. Seating ten passengers, the S.55C and the improved, deeper-hulled S.55P entered service in some numbers. The layout stemmed from the S.55's original role as a torpedo-bomber, the aircraft having been designed to carry torpedoes beneath the uninterrupted wing centre-section. This strange-looking device was powered by a pair of 400 hp Lorraine engines built under licence by Isotta-Fraschini of Milan.

Probably the most successful airliner of the 1920s was a development of the classic Fokker design: the Fokker F.VII was a larger version of the F.III, flown in 1924; it was followed in the next year by the refined Fokker F.VIIa. Both these aircraft had single engines of 400 hp (Jupiter or Liberty units were used), but in September 1925 Fokker flew the F.VIIa/3m with three 200 hp Wright Whirlwinds. This was the first Fokker trimotor, and the main production versions were the F.VIIb/3m of 1928, and its US equivalents.

In the late 1920s and early 1930s most of the European national airlines, excepting those with an established home industry, relied on the Fokker, which could carry its load of ten passengers at slightly under 100 mph. A vast variety of engines

To anyone involved in the airline industry of the late 1920s, the concept of an aircraft capable of carrying literally hundreds of people non-stop for thousands of miles must have seemed even more unlikely than supersonic flight, yet Boeing 747 "Jumbos" – like this Aerolineas Argentinas example – became a common sight in the 1970s

could be fitted, considerably enhancing the attractions of the type. Fokkers were built in the USA, Belgium, Poland, Czechoslovakia, Italy and, as the Avro Ten, in the United Kingdom. Some of the Fokker licensees produced their own variations; this independence was particulary marked in the case of the Fokker Aircraft Corporation of America. Part-owned by General Motors, this concern had been set up to manufacture Fokker designs, but developed some purely-US types as well. The last and biggest of the US-developed Fokkers was the F.32, powered by four 525 hp Pratt & Whitney Hornets and seating 32 passengers. The type was still recognisably a Fokker, with the same type of high-mounted wooden wing and the engines in tandem pairs under the mainplane.

Most of those American airlines who did not operate Fokkers built with the aid of General Motors were operating a similar design built by Ford. The Ford Motor Company had acquired control of the Stout Metal Airplane Company in 1926,

and had commenced production of the three-engined airliner designed by that company's founder, William B. Stout. The original 4AT version of the famous Ford Tri-Motor or "Tin Goose" was similar in dimensions and layout to the Fokker F.VIIb/3m, but was constructed entirely of metal. The slightly larger and heavier 15-passenger 5AT used 420 hp Pratt & Whitney Wasp engines. These Fords and Fokkers dominated the American air routes, although some early Boeing Model 80A three-engined biplanes flew with Boeing's associate, United Air Lines. At that time, the only way in which most of the US routes could be operated, in the absence of direct government subsidies, was via air mail contracts. Many services were thus flown by small mailplanes, with only one or two seats for passengers, and it was the European carriers which set the technical pace.

Germany fell behind in the race with the Dutch after the Fokker trimotors became established, but still enjoyed considerable success with the Junkers all-metal, low-wing

above
Fokker XII built under licence in Denmark and seen here in the colours of a Danish airline

opposite, top
With Wright Cyclone engines, retractable undercarriage and space for 12 passengers, the Fokker F.XX was among the most refined airliners of 1933

opposite, bottom
The wooden-winged Fokker F.VIIB/3m was built in large quantities and was an outstanding aircraft flown with a variety of engines. Designed to carry eight passengers and two crew, the type was flown by many European airlines including Sabena, Ala Littoria, Air Orient, Air France and Swissair

When the Dornier Do X was completed in 1929 it was the largest aeroplane in the world. Originally designed for transatlantic routes, the type never flew on airline service. The Do X could carry 66 passengers on long flights or 100 on short flights but it once carried 169 people

designs. The G.23 and G.24 were the Junkers company's first trimotor designs, but although Lufthansa operated about 20 of the type, many were later converted to single-engined F.24s by the removal of the wing engines and the substitution of a more powerful unit in the nose. Lufthansa clearly considered that the increased risk of an engine failure with a three-engined aircraft offset the advantages of engine-out performance. Another trimotor rather larger in size, was the 15-seater G.31 of 1926. Lufthansa, formed in that year, used G.31s extensively on European routes, with Jupiter and Hornet engines. Junkers' most successful 1920s product, however, was their W.33/34, a freighter variant of the old F.13 with a redesigned fuselage. Nearly 200 W.33s, with a Junkers in-line liquid-cooled engine, were sold, together with 100 radial-engined W.34s with Jupiter or Hornet engines. Used for air photography and crop spraying as well as for freighting, the Junkers freighter saw service throughout the world, particularly in inhospitable and difficult climates.

In 1929, the German industry attracted world attention by flying two vast aircraft, one the world's largest aeroplane, the other the world's largest landplane. First to fly was the 56-ton Dornier Do X flying-boat, which lifted off from the Bodensee in July 1929. Intended for transatlantic operations, the Do X could seat 66 passengers and, as first flown, was powered by no fewer than 12 Siemens-built Jupiters in six tandem pairs above the 157 ft wing. After a few flight tests, it was decided to install 600 hp liquid-cooled Curtiss Conquerors, because of the difficulty of air-cooling the rear engines. After an ardous ten-month Atlantic proving flight, the Do X was relegated to a research institute before being put on display in the Air Museum in Berlin, where it was later destroyed in an air raid. Two Do Xs were built for the Italian airline SANA, but were never operated commercially.

Almost as massive as the Do X was the Junkers G.38, virtually a flying wing in appearance. Professor Junkers was a supporter of the all-wing aircraft, and the G.38 was a forerunner both of wartime Junkers projects and of the massive Ju322 glider of 1941, with the tapered, thick-section wing dwarfing the fuselage. The G.38 was the first aircraft to use the Junkers "double-wing" landing flap or *Hilfsflugel*, which trailed behind the wing in cruising flight and acted as a slotted flap on landing. The engines were almost buried in the wing, which contained cabins for six passengers in the

above
This Ford Tri-Motor was still in regular service with a US internal airline in the 1960s, over three decades after its manufacture. Rumour has it that the Ford engineers had a quiet and careful look at the Fokker trimotor before finalising their designs for the all-metal US aircraft

left
Comparatively luxurious interior of the Ford Tri-Motor with "club" type furnishings

An impressive sight in its day was the giant Junkers G 38 designed by Prof Hugo Junkers and first flown in November 1929. The thick wing section accommodated two passengers either side and the four Junkers water-cooled engines could be attended to in flight. Two of these 30-passenger aircraft were built in Germany and others were licence-built in Japan

leading edge. Two G.38s were built, and one aircraft was still flying in 1940. However, like the Do X, the G.38s mainly proved that the state of the art had not yet made such large aircraft a practical or economic proposition.

In any case, it was felt in many quarters in the 1920s that the airship, not the aeroplane, would be the standard vehicle for long-range, over-water flights. After the First World War, the British airship R.34 had completed a highly successful double Atlantic crossing, at a time when the aeroplane could only with immense difficulty manage a Newfoundland-Ireland crossing on the back of the prevailing winds. The Zeppelin LZ-126 had been completed for the US Navy as the *Los Angeles*, and flew 4,300 hours before its retirement in 1932. The loss of the R.38 in August 1921 caused a momentary dampening of enthusiasm for the airship in Britain, but in late 1923, the Vickers company proposed to the British Government that they should build a fleet of airships more than twice as large as any of the Zeppelins, and operate them on routes which would link the Empire. The British Government responded by issuing a contract to Vickers' subsidiary, the

Airship Guarantee Company for one airship, the R.100, while the Royal Airship Works at Cardington would build a competing ship, the R.101. Production aircraft would be based on whichever design was the more successful.

In 1926, however, the Allies lifted the ban on large airships in Germany, and the Zeppelin company, more experienced than either British concern in the manufacture of large airships, flew the *Graf Zeppelin* in September 1928, over a year ahead of either British ship. The *Graf Zeppelin* was longer but narrower than the British ships as first designed, displacing some 3.7 million cubic feet compared with the 5.6 million cubic feet of the R.100, and it could accommodate 20 passengers in cabins built into the lower part of the hull. The German airship made several commercial crossings of the North Atlantic before setting off on its famous, round-the-world cruise in August and September of 1929. From 1931, the ship undertook regular South Atlantic crossings, setting up the first scheduled transatlantic air service. By the time it was retired in mid-1937, the *Graf Zeppelin* had made 144 Atlantic crossings and had flown more than a million miles.

The R.100 was the first of the two British airships to fly, towards the end of 1929. Powered by six Rolls-Royce Condor petrol engines, the R.100 repeated the R.34's double Atlantic crossing in July-August 1930, flying from Cardington to Montreal in 78 hours and making the downwind return trip in 56 hours.

The maiden voyage of the R.101, by contrast, was delayed by the need for major modifications, including the insertion of a new 44 ft section in the hull to increase the lifting power; among other things, the Beardmore Tornado diesel engines had turned out to be much heavier than expected. Although the R.101 had only flown 16 hours since the modifications, and not all its flight tests had been completed, it was despatched on a maiden voyage to India in October 1930, crashing near Beauvais with heavy loss of life. Among the dead were the Secretary of State for Air, Lord Thomson of Cardington, and the Minister of Civil Aviation, Sir Sefton Brancker, who had been the political driving forces behind the British airship programme. Although the R.100 had shown no serious problems in its trials, the entire programme was cancelled and the R.100 was broken up for scrap.

In 1934, the Zeppelin company began construction of a new airship, larger and faster than the *Graf Zeppelin*, intended for the North Atlantic run. Powered by four 1,050 hp Daimler diesel engines, the LZ-129 was to have a cruising speed of 80 mph and would carry 54 passengers. (After the first season's operations, capacity was increased to 72.). The total volume of the new airship, named *Hindenburg* after the German President, was 6.7 million cubic feet, substantially larger than either British airship. *Hindenburg* made 36 round-trips over the North Atlantic from its first flight in March 1936 to May 1937. On May 6, at the end of its 73rd flight, it caught fire and was destroyed with the loss of 35 lives at Lakehurst, New Jersey. Recorded by a waiting newsreel team, the *Hindenburg* accident spelt the end of the commercial passenger-carrying airship, despite the record of the *Graf Zeppelin*. One more Zeppelin, the LZ-130 *Graf Zeppelin II*, was built, but never went into service.

The development of the giant passenger airship had thus proved abortive, and it was to be with aeroplanes that regular air links between the continents were established.

Last of the great rigid airships was the LZ-130 *Graf Zeppelin II*, never put into scheduled service

America surges ahead

The early 1930s saw a complete reversal in the fortunes of the airline industries of the United States and Europe. The reasons were varied, but the story was one of conservatism in the Old World and of inititative and innovation in the New.

In November 1930, what was then the ultimate in airliners made its maiden flight from Handley Page's airfield at Radlett, North of London. The HP.42 was a giant in overall dimensions, its upper wing spanning 130 ft, and was a mixture of old and new. The structure was all-metal with fabric skinning on the wings and rear fuselage; it was a biplane, but with diagonal Warren strutting which eliminated bracing wires, and the upper wing was markedly larger than the lower. Two of the four Bristol Jupiters were carried close together on the upper wing, minimising engine-out control problems. Imperial Airways and Handley Page had designed the HP.42 for passenger comfort first and foremost, together with low-speed characteristics as good as those of the early biplanes. Speed was quite clearly a secondary consideration; with its bracing struts, biplane tail and uncowled engines, the HP.42 could cruise at a stately 100 mph if pressed.

Only a handful of HP.42s were built: the HP.42E *Hannibal*-class aircraft were used on Imperial Airways' Eastern routes from Cairo to Karachi and Cape Town, seating 18 passengers; the HP.42W *Heracles*-class carried up to 38 passengers on European flights. The HP.42s flew without a single fatal accident until 1940, when *Hannibal* vanished over the Indian Ocean.

Slightly more modern in concept were the eight Armstrong Whitworth Atalantas, built in 1931–32 for the "hot-and-high" airfields of the Karachi-Singapore and Nairobi-Cape Town routes. The Atalanta was a high-wing monoplane, with four twin-row radials wrapped in Townend ring cowlings to improve cooling and reduce drag. (The multi-row radial was to become the standard airliner powerplant for the next 25 years, offering more power per unit of frontal area than the single-row engine.)

Third of the new types to emerge in Europe in 1930–32 was to be the only European transport of the 1930s to hold its own against the American invasion. Junkers had flown the first Ju52 in October 1930, this being a large, single-engined freighter and airliner designed to use a powerplant in the 750–800 hp class. Ju52s were tested with BMW, Rolls-Royce and Junkers engines. The Junkers double-wing flap, seen on the giant G.38, extended over the full span.

In April 1932, the first modified version of the Ju52 made its maiden flight: the three-engined Ju52/3m. More than 5,000 of these *Tante Ju* (Auntie Ju) airliners, freighters and bombers were to be built, and it was with a fleet of 50 of these safe, reliable aircraft that Lufthansa maintained their European operations throughout the 1930s, later German landplane airliners being more notable for their military potential than for their commercial

practicability. The better field performance of the Ju52/3m compared
with the later American twins ensured its acceptability in the "difficult" areas of the world before the
US airliners were widely operated
outside their country of origin. Many
of the emerging South American
airlines operated the rugged Junkers.
Even after 1945, British European
Airways and Air France introduced
the Ju52, the French carrier operating French-built AAC.1 versions.
Most of the German-built Ju52s were
powered by the 525 hp BMW 132
radials.

The Depression had caused something of a revolution in the US
manufacturing industry, and the
effects of this were to be far-reaching.

During the slump, both Ford and
General Motors had withdrawn from
aeroplane manufacture, so that there
were no evolutionary replacements
for the Fords or the American-built
Fokkers. The field was left clear for
three new companies, none of which
had been deeply involved in airliner manufacture before: Boeing,
Douglas and Lockheed invaded the
market to such effect that they were
to dominate the airliner business for
the next 50 years.

One US airliner of the early 1930s,
however, reflected developments in
Europe: the Curtiss Condor was a
large and somewhat portly equal-
span biplane, developed for
American Airlines, and entering
service in 1933. Its career was short,

Only four years separated the first flights of these two aircraft: The 24-passenger Handley Page H.P.42 cruised at a leisurely 95 mph; The Swissair DC-2 carried 14 passengers at twice the speed on three quarters of the power

the Condor being retired from first-line service with American in 1936–37, but it displayed at least three significant features. The first was a retractable undercarriage, applied for the first time to a large airliner; the second was its intended role as a sleeper transport, a concept which was to inspire the development of the DC-3; the third was its use of the Wright R-1820 Cyclone, a single-row nine-cylinder unit, then rated at 550 hp, but later to yield 1,000 hp for early DC-3s.

The Condor was overtaken by a new development from the Boeing company. Boeing had successfully struggled for existence building fighters through the 1920s, and in 1926 had bid successfully for a US Air Mail route. Boeing Air Transport, later to become United Airlines, operated specially-built Boeing 40B single-engined mail-planes, biplanes with room for two passengers in addition to the mail. The company also built the 18-seater Boeing 80A trimotor but the type was too large for year-round use on the long airmail routes.

Speed was clearly of the essence on the airmail service, and all the mailplane builders were looking at faster aircraft. Boeing built a single prototype of their Monomail, a revolutionary design which owed more to racing aircraft than to previous transports. The Monomail was a single-engined design, which featured retractable undercarriage, a long-chord NACA cowling and a smooth metal skin which, for the

first time, carried the main flight loads. Flown in May 1930, the Monomail was in many ways ahead of its time; in particular, no variable-pitch propeller was available when it was built, and the design of its propeller was thus an awkward compromise between the demands of low-speed power (needed for good take-off performance) and high-speed cruise. The Monomail was never put into production, but the lessons learned from its construction were embodied in the design of Boeing's experimental B-9 bomber, and the wing of the B-9 was used for a new airliner, with which Boeing and United Air Lines hoped to dominate the airways.

The Boeing 247, flown in early 1933, could carry ten passengers at the astonishing cruising speed of 180 mph, nearly twice as fast as the Fords and Fokkers then in service. United ordered 60 of the new aircraft, and Boeing told other airline customers that they would have to wait for 247s until the United order was completed.

Transcontinental and Western Air (TWA, later Trans World Airlines) had been commercially linked to the Fokker Aircraft Corporation until GM severed their aviation connections in 1931. Worried that their arch-rivals United would drive them out of business with their monopoly of the 247, TWA issued a specification in 1932 for an aircraft of similar performance, powered by three 550 hp Pratt & Whitney Wasps.

above
Looking rather like a biplane version of the Douglas DC-2, the Curtiss T-32 Condor was a 15-seater powered by two 700 hp Wright Cyclones. Some of Eastern Air Transport's Condors were sold to Britain, where they were converted into freighters

left
The interior of the one and only DC-1 delivered to TWA in February 1934; 12 passengers, a crew of two and 1,000 lb of freight could be accommodated

The relatively small Douglas company, whose most successful product so far had been the small Dolphin amphibian, studied the specification and decided that a twin-engined aircraft would be better than a trimotor, now that it was known that the Wright R-1820 could be developed to yield more than 700 hp. This was considerably more than the output of the Wasps on the 247, allowing Douglas to use a bigger fuselage cross-section for their design while matching the Boeing's speed. Like the 247, the Douglas design drew inspiration from single-engined types, notably a series of Northrop record-breaking and research monoplanes. The wing structure was based on Northrop ideas, with outer wings bolted to a centre section which combined the fuselage with stub wings. In the 247, the continuous mainspar interrupted the cabin and Douglas were determined to avoid this. The trailing edges of the wing carried simple split flaps.

In September 1932, TWA ordered a single prototype designated DC-1, on the strict condition that it should demonstrate engine-out performance comparable to that of a tri-

Douglas were among the first companies to appreciate the potential of passenger air travel, and they introduced the DC-1 in 1933. By the time their numbering system had reached -10, the company were making giant jets like this DC-10-30 operated by Canadian charter line Wardair

motor. On its first flight in July 1933, the DC-1 nearly crashed due to an unforeseen engine problem, but subsequent trials were successful enough to warrant a TWA order for a slightly stretched version of the aircraft, seating 14 passengers and designated DC-2. Orders for the DC-2 rapidly followed from Pan American, Eastern, Western, Braniff and Northwest. United's smaller, more cramped 247s were outclassed, despite the development of the improved 247D. In the year the DC-2 entered service (1934), the US Congress decided that airlines should no longer be associated with airliner manufacturers, and this immediately freed United from the need to buy Boeing.

The first DC-1 and the early production DC-2s were hand-built to a far greater degree than later aircraft, because the rapid expansion of the small Douglas company had left no time for tooling-up on a more extensive scale. Many of the sheet-metal components were hand-

formed, and early aircraft took more manhours to build than the company had planned. It was therefore with some reluctance that, in mid-1934, Douglas agreed to build a bigger version of the DC-2 for American Airlines.

American had pioneered sleeper services with the Curtiss Condor, and the new version of the DC-2 was to be the Condor's replacement. The new Douglas Sleeper Transport (DST) was envisaged by American as a fairly straightforward derivative of the DC-2 with the new 1,000 hp R-1820s and a fatter fuselage, big enough to take two tiers of berths on each side for a total sleeper capacity of 14 passengers. However, such was the effect of the wider body on the handling and performance of the aircraft that the DST emerged as an almost completely different aircraft in detail, although it bore a close resemblance to its predecessor. The tail shape was different, and the characteristic sweepback of the DC-2 wing became more pronounced, eliminating the slight instability which characterised the DC-2.

Flown in December 1935, the original American Airlines DST was powered by 1,050 hp Wright R-1820 Cyclones. Pratt & Whitney, however, had not been idle, and the DSTs ordered by United had 14-cylinder, two-row R-1830 Twin Wasps. The Pratt & Whitney engine was to become the most commonly used engine on the new aircraft, and powered all its military descendants.

TWA placed the first order for the 21-passenger daytime version of the DST, designated DC-3. This version accounted for most of the 803 airline sales of the type, sleeper services proving to be a passing phase: by 1940, US airlines were committed to greater speed rather than sleeper accommodation on their trans-continental services.

The DC-3 was a classic well before the Second World War, when massive production of the C-47 Skytrain (known as the Dakota to Britain's Royal Air Force) took total production to over 13,000 and created a force of aircraft which, after the war, took air transport all over the world. The rapid expansion of the US airlines during the second half of the 1930s was largely attributable to the Douglas twins.

This expansion necessitated tighter government regulation of airliner airworthiness and airline economics. The 1938 Civil Aeronautics Act set up the Civil Aeronautics Authority (CAA) which fulfilled these functions for many years until it was split into the Civil Aeronautics Board, dealing with route licensing, and the Federal Aviation Administration, dealing with airworthiness and operational standards. Also formed in 1938 was the Air Safety Board, independent of the CAA and required to investigate accidents and comment on the CAA'S performance. The standards for aircraft performance laid down by the CAA were based on those of the DC-2. The CAA were also responsible for the development and installation of radio beacons and blind-landing equipment.

The shape of the US airline industry became largely set during

the late 1930s. Pan American became virtually the national carrier, with first call on international routes. TWA, American and United became locked in deadly rivalry over the key transcontinental routes, while Eastern concentrated on the Atlantic seaboard. At that time, Braniff and Western (now among the smaller "trunk" airlines) were more like today's regional airlines.

In the US manufacturing stakes, a third contender, Lockheed, came close to disturbing the Douglas dominance in the immediate pre-war years. The company had built a series of cantilever wooden monoplane transports and record-breakers starting in 1927, culminating in the low-wing, single-engined Orion of 1931. The Orion was the fastest airliner of its day, with a retractable undercarriage and a 200 mph cruising speed. However, in 1931 the holding company which owned Lockheed failed, and the company was acquired by Robert Gross, a San

top
Perhaps the most famous transport aeroplane of all time, the Douglas DC-3 was built in quantity at Santa Monica, California from 1936. The type is likely to remain in service well into the 1980s, outlasting many "DC-3 replacements"

above
The Lockheed Orion was the fastest airliner in the world when it entered service. This Swissair example was pictured in 1930

31

Francisco businessman. Gross put the Orion into production, and at the same time started development of an all-metal, ten-seat twin which became the Lockheed 10 Electra. Smaller and cheaper than the DC-2, the Electra found a place in many fleets. Nearly 150 were built, together with 114 scaled-down eight-seat Lockheed 12s, intended mainly as executive transports.

Lockheed had more ambitious plans, too, and in July 1937 flew the prototype Lockheed 14, sometimes known as the Super Electra. It was a 14-seater, like the DC-2, but had more power and a smaller, more advanced wing. It was also the first airliner to carry area-increasing

Fowler flaps, which combined the slow-flying qualities of the Junkers double-wing with virtually no cruise drag. A distinguishing feature of the 14 was the row of flap-tracks jutting from the trailing-edge of the wing. With its high wing loading and more power than the DC-2 (from 820 hp versions of the proven Wright R-1820, although some 14s had Pratt & Whitney engines), the 14 could cruise at 237 mph, 30 mph faster than the DC-3. After the sale of 112 of the type, Lockheed offered the model 18 Lodestar, stretched to seat 17 passengers and with a slightly modified wing and tail to cure flutter problems, but only 54 were delivered before the Second World War broke out. The 14 became the basis for the Hudson patrol bomber used by RAF Coastal Command, while the 18 became the US Navy's Ventura and Harpoon.

The Douglas company's attempt to counter the Lockheed 14 was uncharacteristically fruitless. The 16-seat DC-5, with its high wing and nosewheel undercarriage, proved substantially heavier than the Lockheed aircraft when it flew in early in 1939. Four were ordered by KLM, and were operated in the East and West Indies; of the East Indies-based aircraft, one was captured by the Japanese, while the two Antilles-based aircraft eventually joined six other DC-5s in military service.

The Boeing, Lockheed and – above all – Douglas developments had left the European industry in the Stone Age. The Fokker company were the first to realise that the development of the Boeing 247 and DC-2 was opening a vast technology gap which Europe could not hope to close. In 1933, Fokker were working on the F.XX for KLM; although this was much cleaner and faster than previous Fokker designs, with a circular-section fuselage, retractable undercarriage and NACA cowlings, it retained the thick, wooden, high-set wing and was outclassed by the DC-2, which was only marginally smaller, despite having only two Wright R-1820s instead of three. Anthony Fokker saw the DC-2 in 1933 and signed an

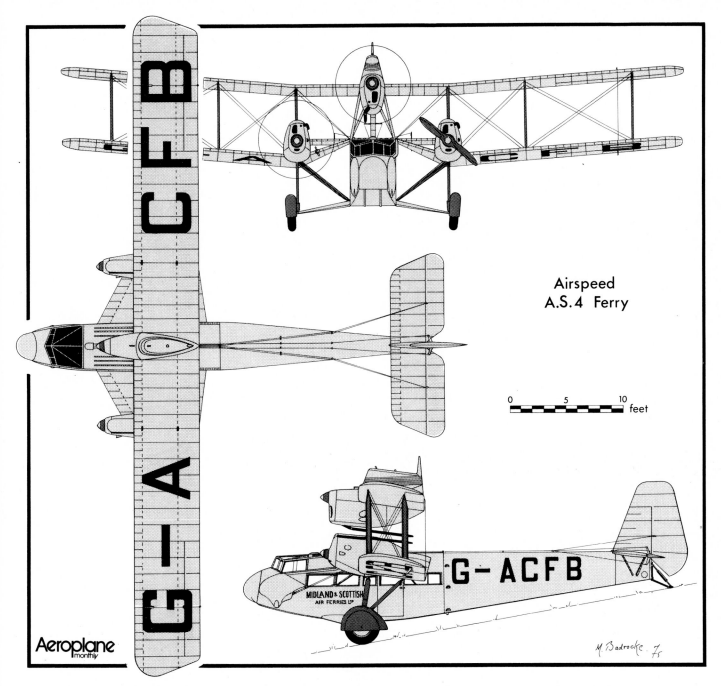

Airspeed
A.S.4 Ferry

0   5   10 feet

M. Badrocke. 75

Aeroplane
monthly

agreement to build the type under licence. With Fokker backing, KLM decided to re-equip with the DC-2, and took delivery of their first two Douglas-built aircraft in 1934. Only one Fokker F.XX was built, and thereafter the only pre-war airliners of Fokker design were four 22-seat F.XXIIs and just one 36-seat F.XXXVI, all four-engined, high-wing aircraft with fixed landing gear. The F.XXXVI was designed for KLM's Far East routes, but the Dutch carrier operated DC-2s on these services instead.

The British industry woke up to the capabilities of the DC-2 after the London-Melbourne Air Race in October 1934. The race was won by

a British aircraft, the specially built two-seat de Havilland Comet racer, but second place fell to an entirely standard KLM DC-2. A few months earlier, Imperial Airways had introduced two Short L.17 Scylla-class airliners, massive and awkward machines derived from the Short Kent flying-boat, itself an enlarged, four-engined version of the 1928 Calcutta. To be fair, the 40-seat Scylla was specifically designed for the short London-Paris and London-Brussels flights, but its cruising speed was no higher than that of the HP.42.

The de Havilland company, whose commercial activities in the early 1930s had centred on development of the highly successful six-seat

The Airspeed A.S.4 Ferry was a three-engined design intended for feeder line service. Although the ten-seater aircraft worked well, the anticipated demand for orders was never realised and only a few were ever completed

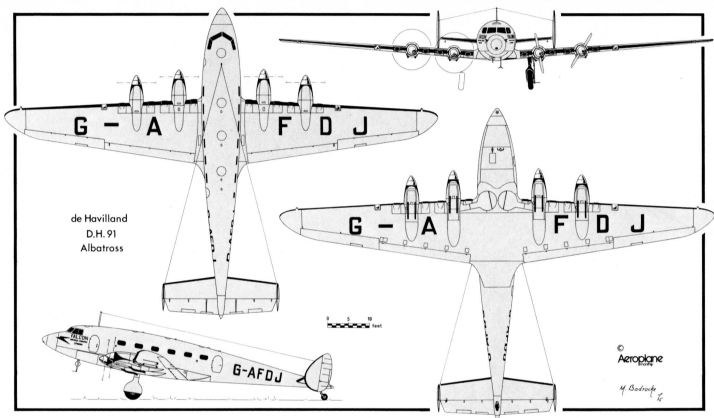

de Havilland
D.H. 91
Albatross

G-AFDJ

0   5   10
feet

© Aeroplane monthly

M. Badrocke '76

top
Two Lockheed designs which typify the state of the art in the late 1930s: a ten-seat Electra 10 (right) and a smaller, eight-seat 12A.

above
One of the most aesthetically pleasing aeroplanes of its day was de Havilland's D.H.91 Albatross. Its sleek lines helped to give a cruising speed of 210 mph. Powered by four 525 hp de Havilland Gipsy Twelve engines, Imperial Airways operated passenger and mail flights on the Croydon to Paris, Brussels and Zurich routes. Only seven were built

D.H.84 Dragon light transport, the four-engined D.H.86 and the refined D.H.89A Rapide, did at least react to the DC-2. Only weeks after the England-Australia race, de Havillands proposed a high-speed airliner of great aerodynamic refinement, and, in May 1937, this flew as the de Havilland D.H.91 Albatross. The Albatross was full of advanced features. The four inverted V-12 Gipsy Twelve engines were air-cooled by a reverse-flow system, cooling air entering through intakes in the leading edge of the wing and passing forward through the almost perfectly streamlined cowling. The

wing was of high aspect ratio and unusually thin section; above all, the entire aircraft was made of wood, a plywood and balsa sandwich being used for the stressed skin. Two variants of the Albatross existed, one being a transatlantic mailplane, the other a 22-seat *Frobisher*-class airliner of Imperial Airways. The Albatross entered airline service in October 1938, but later wartime service was cut short by structural problems. The wooden construction of the Albatross was later refined and adapted for the famous Mosquito. Another airliner of pre-war de Havilland design was the D.H.95

G-AKIF

Flamingo, a high-wing aircraft comparable in size and power with the Lockheed 14, but considerably slower.

Britain's first large aircraft of stressed-skin construction was the Armstrong Whitworth AW.27 Ensign, a 40-seater airliner superficially similar to the Atalanta, with the same high wing, but with a retractable undercarriage. Fourteen Ensigns were built, entering service with Imperial Airways in October 1938, but the type, which used four Armstrong Siddeley Tiger engines, was somewhat underpowered.

From 1936, Imperial Airways faced competition from the original British Airways, formed by the merger of a group of small independent carriers. In 1936, finding their de Havilland biplanes too slow, British Airways ordered five Lockheed 10s, following these with eight of the larger Lockheed 14s. All of these aircraft were faster than anything that Imperial Airways could offer. British Airways was merged with Imperial Airways in 1940 to form the British Overseas Airways Corporation.

In the Germany of 1933, there was little question of importing foreign aircraft of any description, but the

Mainstay of world commercial aviation for two decades was the De Havilland D.H.89 Dragon Rapide. It remained in production for ten years and a total of 728 were built

Less than a dozen Junkers Ju 90s were delivered to Deutsche Lufthansa. Designed to carry 38–40 passengers, large scale operation of the type was prevented by the war. Illustrated here is the prototype, which was destroyed during flutter tests in February 1938

development of airliners was hampered by the insistence of the Air Ministry that the same basic airframes should be produced in airliner and bomber versions. Examples of this policy were the Heinkel He111 and Junkers Ju86, both ordered in bomber and transport versions in 1934. Neither proved successful in airline service, largely because their fuselages were too cramped for comfortable passenger accommodation. Lufthansa had six He111s and ten Ju86s, but continued to use the trusty Ju52/3m for the bulk of their traffic. However, two South American carriers and South African Airways ordered Ju86s.

The Ju86 was interesting in that it was the only landplane airliner to go into production with diesel engines. The Junkers Jumo 205 was a highly unorthodox engine, having a single row of six cylinders with 12 pistons and a crankshaft at either end. It was a two-stroke engine, fitted with a mechanical blower to drive burnt gases out of the cylinders. Compared with a piston engine it was heavier but consumed less fuel, making it more suitable for long-range aircraft than for a short-haul airliner like the Ju86. South African Airways fitted Pratt & Whitney Hornets to their Ju86s.

Lufthansa also operated two single-engined high-speed transports, the Heinkel He70 Blitz and the Junkers Ju160, in small numbers on special services. Brought into service in mid-1934, both were clean, low-wing designs of all-metal construction, with retractable landing gear. The Dornier Do17 bomber

was also initially developed as a high-speed special transport for Lufthansa, but was rejected because of its hopelessly cramped interior.

Two further European-range airliners were designed for Lufthansa, neither of them attaining large-scale service. The four-engined Ju90 was a development of the Ju89 bomber, Junkers having sought permission to complete the third Ju89 prototype as an airliner after the Luftwaffe cancelled its *Ural-Bomber* programme in 1937. The 40-seat Ju90V1, powered by Jumo diesels, was flown in August 1937 but crashed early in the following year. Two further prototypes and eight production aircraft, powered by BMW air-cooled radials, were completed before the programme was diverted to the production of military aircraft. The last landplane designed for the prewar Lufthansa was the Ju252, a 35-seater trimotor bearing no more than a family resemblance to the much smaller Ju52/3m. However, the type was earmarked as a military transport even before the prototype flew.

The rest of Europe remained insular, each nation meeting its own needs. Air France and their predecessor Air Union relied heavily on Wibault fixed-gear trimotor monoplanes until the mid-1930s, but as late as mid-1934, Air France introduced the first of six Breguet 393T three-engine biplanes. More advanced was the Bloch 220 (produced by the firm which later became Dassault), which was strongly reminiscent of the DC-2. Powered by two Gnome-Rhone 14N radials, the 220 could carry 16 passengers. Some of the 16 built for Air France from 1936 onwards were commandeered by the Germans and used by Lufthansa from 1943 onwards. After the war, five of the surviving 220s were modified to Bloch 221s by the installation of Wright R-1820s.

Air France's most advanced pre-war type, however, was the three-engined Dewoitine D.338 introduced in 1936. Powered by three Hispano-Suiza-built Cyclones, the D.338 carried up to 22 passengers on European routes and about 30 were built for Air France. The D.338 was a more powerful, retractable-gear version of the D.333, of which three had been built in 1934.

Italy commenced production of two families of landplane airliners in the early 1930s. The most abundant was the series of airliners produced by Savoia-Marchetti, previously noted as a manufacturer of marine aircraft. The first of the series, the ten-seat, three-engined S.71, flew in 1930 and was followed by the S.73, an 18-seater trimotor sold to Sabena and CSA as well as to the Italian carriers ATI and Ala Littoria. The largest of the pre-war series was the 30-seater SM.75, which introduced a retractable landing gear. A float-plane version was designated SM.87

and used by Ala Littoria. In 1937, there appeared the longer-range SM.83, developed from the S.79 Sparviero bomber. The last of the family was the SM.95, a 38-seater with four engines, which did not fly until May 1943 and entered service after the war. Also produced in some numbers were the Fiat G.12 tri-motor and the scaled-up, 34-seat G.212, which also entered service with Alitalia after 1945.

In the 1930s, the Soviet Union moved to reduce her dependence on imported aircraft. Aeroflot expanded their operations with the help of 260 single-engined, high-wing Kalinin K-5 monoplanes built between 1930 and 1934. Rather larger than the K-5 was A N Tupolev's ANT-9 trimotor, of which about 70 were built. Tupolev's design team were also responsible for some very large experimental transport aircraft. The first of these was the 36-seater, five-engined ANT-14, flown in 1931. In general appearance, it echoed the slab-sided, massive appearance of Tupolev's giant TB-3 strategic bomber. Dwarfing even the ANT-14, however, was the gigantic ANT-20. Flown in July 1934, the ANT-20 spanned 206 ft and was powered by eight 1,000 hp liquid-cooled engines, six of them buried in

A Savoia Marchetti S.73 operated by Sabena and powered by three 600 hp Gnome-Rhône Mistral Major engines. The fuselage was built of fabric covered steel tubing but the wings were of wood, covered with ply

The eight-engined ANT-20 *Maxim Gorki* first flew in May 1934 and was used mainly for propaganda work until destroyed during a mid-air collision with a light aircraft. An improved version, the six-engined ANT-20bis, was built and probably flown on the Moscow-Mineral'nyye Vody service during the early part of the Second World War

the wing leading edge and two more mounted back-to-back above the fuselage. Passenger cabins in the wings and fuselage could accommodate 72 people. The ANT-20 was destroyed in a mid-air collision in May 1935, but was followed in 1939 by the ANT-20bis, similar in dimensions and capacity but powered by six 1,200 hp engines. The ANT-20bis was employed on an experimental service between Moscow and Mineral'nye Vody in 1940–41.

Notwithstanding the progress made in the design of the landplane in the early 1930s, there were many who believed that the apparently irreversible tendency for runway length to increase with aircraft size would rule out the use of land-based aircraft for long-haul routes. Just as the airship was the favourite for long-range services in the late 1920s, so the flying-boat was considered to be the solution in the 1930s. It was the crossings of the North and South Atlantic which attracted most attention and interest. Charles Lindbergh's New York-Paris flight of May 1927 attracted massive public attention, but at that time no aeroplane had even managed the relatively short Ireland-Newfoundland crossing in the reverse direction, the slow cruising speeds of the day accentuating the effect of the prevailing headwinds. It was a Junkers W.33 which first achieved this feat in April 1928, and – in September 1930, less than two-and-a-half years

later – a highly modified Breguet 19 flew all the way from Paris to New York. Three years later, the North Atlantic was crossed in both directions by a formation of 24 twin-hull Savoia-Marchetti S.55X flying-boats led by General Italo Balbo. Clearly it was only a matter of time before regular mail service across the Atlantic became possible by air.

There was keen rivalry between France's Aeropostale and Germany's Lufthansa to be the first to fly South Atlantic mail services all the way down to South America, eliminating the surface-ship sector between West Africa and Brazil. In fact it was Lufthansa which inaugurated the first regular aeroplane service across the Atlantic, using Dornier Wal flying-boats catapulted from a depot ship. The technique had been developed in 1932–33; the flying-boat taxied on to a slipway towed behind the ship, was picked up by a crane, refuelled and launched by steam catapult at a weight considerably higher than its unaided take-off weight from water. Lufthansa Wals made 24 successful crossings of the South Atlantic in 1934, by which time Aeropostale's southern mail service was complete, the over-water sector being flown by two specially designed aircraft, the Couzinet 71 *Arc-en-Ciel* three-engined landplane and the Latécoère 300 *Croix-du-Sud*, a four-engined flying-boat.

Not surprisingly, the lead on the North Atlantic was taken by Britain

and North America. Pan American had acquired a series of progressively larger flying-boats since 1928, when they put their first Sikorsky S.38s into service. (Igor Sikorsky, designer of *Le Grand* in St Petersburg in 1913, had become an *emigré* with the Revolution, specialising in marine aircraft. Later, his company switched completely to helicopter development.) In 1931, Pan Am introduced the S.40, a scaled-up version of the S.38 seating 40 passengers and powered by four Pratt & Whitney Hornets rather than two. Like the S.38, it carried its monoplane wing high above the hull and outrigged stabilising floats, the tail being carried on a boom projecting from the wing. The engines were carried between the hull and the wing. In August 1934, Pan Am introduced the first trans-oceanic Sikorsky, the S.42. A much cleaner and heavier aeroplane than the many-strutted

S.40, the S.42 carried its wing above the hull on a faired pylon, with four engines smoothly faired into the leading edge. It was with S.42s that Pan Am carried out their first North Atlantic proving flights in July 1937. Meanwhile, the airline had put three even bigger Martin 130s into service across the Pacific.

Meanwhile, in 1935, Imperial Airways had ordered 28 flying-boats of a very advanced design, following a Government decision to carry all mail by air. The new aircraft, the Short S.23, was to replace all the landplanes used on the great eastbound route to Australia. It was a clean, cantilever monoplane grossing 40,500 lb for take-off, with a full-depth hull and capacity for 16 sleeper passengers and 3,500 lb of mail. Powerplants were four Bristol Pegasus radials of 920 hp; aerodynamically, the new boats were probably the cleanest flown at that

The Short-Mayo composite. The seaplane Mercury is launched from Maia, a specially equipped Short Empire Class flying boat.

time. The S.23s and the later S.30s were known as the C-class to Imperial Airways, the first aircraft, *Canopus*, being flown in July 1936. By February 1937, the C-class had taken over from the landplanes, but there is cause to wonder if Imperial Airways were not a little hasty with the introduction of the radical new craft; no fewer than eight of the final total of 31 S.23s were lost in major fatal accidents during the first two years of operations. Two of the C-class were built with higher weights and more fuel than the standard aircraft, and these made Imperial Airways' first transatlantic proving flights in 1938. Like the Pan Am S.42s, the British aircraft took the southerly route, landing at Lisbon and the Azores.

German airmail operations on the North Atlantic had started in the late 1920s. Small single-engine floatplanes were carried on the liners Bremen and Europa, and were catapulted as soon as the ships were within range of the US coast, saving a few days in the transport of urgent mail. On arrival at New York, the

seaplane was re-embarked, and the process was repeated on the return voyage. During 1934, the service averaged one launch every ten days.

In 1936, Lufthansa installed the depot ship *Schwabenland* between the Azores and carried out a series of experimental flights using the Do18, a new flying-boat sharing the basic layout of the venerable Wal and powered by Junkers diesels. In the following year, the larger catapult ship *Friesenland* came into service, and launched the new Blohm & Voss Ha139 floatplane on a series of seven double crossings to New York. By this time, Do18s had taken over the South Atlantic service, and in 1938 one of them set a distance record for seaplanes after a launch from the *Westfalen*.

In the event, it was only the lack of a bilateral agreement with the USA that prevented Lufthansa from starting the first North Atlantic heavier-than-air mail service. Dornier designed the sleek Do26 for the Atlantic routes, and the first of these flying-boats flew in May 1938. Four Jumo diesels were carried in

opposite, top
A Handley Page H.P.54 Harrow II short range tanker aircraft refuelling a Short S.30 flying boat over Southampton Water in July 1939

opposite, bottom
A Dornier Wal leaves the *Schwabenland's* catapult in the South Atlantic after refuelling at its floating base en route for South America. Note the cradle which carried the aircraft, and the stowed crane which hoisted it aboard, left

below
A Dornier Do 26 suspended from the *Ostmark's* crane. The type was the first to be fitted with retractable wing floats and was powered by four Junkers Jumo diesel engines mounted in tandem pairs

tandem pairs above the gull wing. Six Do26s were built, but were pressed into Luftwaffe service on the outbreak of war. In September 1937, Lufthansa ordered three massive 45-ton Bv222 Wiking six-engined boats from Blohm & Voss, but the war ended all hope of a transatlantic air service with these craft.

If Lufthansa's approach to the Atlantic mail was unorthodox, that of Imperial Airways was more so, yet both made use of the fact that an aircraft can fly with a greater load than it can lift off the surface unaided. In July 1938, the first mail was carried by an aeroplane across the North Atlantic: the aeroplane was the Short floatplane *Mercury*, carried aloft from Foynes, Ireland, on the back of the mother-ship *Maia*. *Mercury* was specially designed, while *Maia* was an extensively altered relative of the C-class.

However, it was Pan American Airways' more conventional approach that eventually carried the day. In June 1936, the airline ordered six Boeing 314 flying-boats,

using a modified version of the 152 ft wing designed for Boeing's XB-15 bomber. Weighing 84,000 lb and powered by four 1,600 hp Wright R-2600s, the 314 could tackle Newfoundland-Ireland or New York-Azores with a commercial payload, and went into service in mid-1939. Imperial Airways responded by using two C-class boats equipped for in-flight refuelling, in conjunction with Handley Page Harrow tankers, but the Pan American operation was clearly more practical. After the outbreak of war, three of Pan American's eventual order for 12 Boeing 314s were delivered to BOAC. Imperial Airways' own Short G-class boats, strongly resembling the C-class but half as heavy again and powered by Bristol Hercules engines of 1,380 hp, were too late for regular airline service and were requisitioned as maritime patrol aircraft. The C-class itself became the basis for the highly successful Sunderland.

Air France carried out a number of proving flights across the North

above
The Boeing 314, designed to meet Pan American Airways' requirement for a transoceanic transport, made its first flight on June 7, 1938 and became the largest production airliner in regular airline service. Three were operated by BOAC. The 314 could carry 74 passengers or 40 sleepers, in addition to a crew of ten, and was powered by four 1,600 hp Wright Cyclone radial engines

opposite, top
The S-42 *Flying Clipper* was used by Pan American in 1937 to prove their proposed North Atlantic routes. Similar aircraft saw service on Pan-Am Pacific services

opposite, bottom
The Bloch 161 first flew in September 1939 but Air France were unable to take delivery until 1946, by which time the 161 had become the SNCASE SE.161, being built by Société Nationale des Constructions Aéronautiques du Sud-Ouest. A total of 100 Languedocs were built and Air France were still using the type of in the mid-1950s

Atlantic with the Latécoère 521 flying-boat, a large six-engined craft. The even bigger Latécoère 631, corresponding to Germany's Bv222, was not completed until after the Second World War. Powered by six R-2600s, the 188 ft-span boat was operated experimentally by Air France but never entered service. At the outbreak of war, France was testing the Centre N.223.4, an experimental land-based transatlantic mailplane. Powered by four engines in tandem pairs beneath the wings, the N.223.4 carried all its fuel in the fuselage and was unpressurised, despite the fact that it was intended for operations at high altitudes. The first of three examples flew in March 1939, and no transatlantic flights were ever made. One of the N.223.4s later became the first allied aircraft to bomb Berlin, using its long range to approach the target from the north.

Perhaps the most significant pre-war Atlantic crossing was made in August 1938, however. Some two years previously, the technical direc-

tor of the Focke-Wulf company, Dr Kurt Tank, discussed with Lufthansa a proposal for a four-engined landplane airliner with transatlantic range. The first Fw200 Condor flew in July 1937, and in August the following year a Condor flew non-stop from Berlin to New York, the first transatlantic crossing by a purpose-built, long-range passenger airliner.

Only four Condors were delivered to Lufthansa, and in years to come the type was to be remembered not as an airliner but as the maritime reconnaissance aircraft that led Germany's U-boats to their prey. The Second World War also saw the mass Atlantic ferry flights which brought US-built aircraft to Britain, and the establishment of regular Atlantic air services for high-priority freight and mail by C-87 Liberators and C-54 Skymasters. It also saw the final acceptance of the 7,000 ft concrete runways which the heavily laden landplanes required. The brief heyday of the flying-boat had passed.

The great piston airliners

The ubiquitous DC-3 was possibly the last of the all-purpose airliners. By the time it entered service with the US airlines, they were already talking to the manufacturers about a new generation of aircraft, bigger than the Douglas twin and better suited to the longer transcontinental routes.

Part of the spur for new developments came from the realisation that an airliner could cruise more efficiently if its cruising height was increased. Moreover, an airliner flying at 20,000 ft or more would be above much of the weather, giving passengers a far more comfortable ride than the DC-3. Such an aircraft could be a powerful competitive weapon for the airlines; this was particularly attractive to United Air Lines, American and TWA, the three leading contenders for trans-USA traffic. The passenger appeal of the DC-3, with its fast, transcontinental sleeper flights, had already led to expanded traffic, and early fears that the airlines could not support so large an aircraft had therefore been allayed.

However, the design of a high-flying airliner would demand the introduction of a pressurised cabin, a technical innovation which had not even been test-flown at the time the DC-3 went into service. Early high-altitude research flights had been made with the aid of cumbersome pressure suits for the pilots. The idea of pumping air into a sealed cabin, using engine-driven superchargers, was a logical one, but it presented numerous practical problems. The most serious was the enormous strain put on the fuselage structure, particularly around doors and windows.

The first aircraft to fly with a pressurised cabin suitable for carrying passengers was the Lockheed XC-35, an Electra modified under a US Army Air Corps contract requiring a pressurised cabin. The powerplants were Pratt & Whitney R-1340s fitted with turbo-superchargers – air was pumped into the engines by a compressor driven by an exhaust turbine. (Although turbocharging was used on most of the USA's wartime heavy bombers, most piston airliners had simple superchargers driven directly from the engines.) The XC-35 flew in May 1937, and Lockheed's experience with its pressure cabin proved in-

valuable in their development of the Constellation.

Boeing, meanwhile, were extricating themselves from the hard times on which they had fallen after the 247 was overtaken by the DC-2 and DC-3. A US Government action of 1934 broke the links between Boeing and United Air Lines by separating both from their holding company, United Aircraft. The change of ownership left Boeing with insufficient funds to develop a direct competitor to the DC-3, and the company began to look instead at the potential of a four-engined bomber and a similar transport. The Boeing 299 bomber, forerunner of the famous B-17 Flying Fortress, was built first for a 1935 USAAC (United States Army Air Corps) bomber competition, and – although it was destroyed during the "fly-off" evaluation – the USAAC ordered a few aircraft for further tests.

In mid-1936, Boeing proposed an airliner derivative, the pressurised Model 307, to Pan Am and TWA. The turbocharged Wright R-1820 engines and the wing of the 299 were married to a circular-section, teardrop-shaped fuselage with a

above
Originally designed as a pressurised airliner, the Curtiss CW-20 was first put into service as the C-46 military freighter. After the war, many were sold to the airlines

left
The Boeing Model 307 Stratoliner was a transport version of the B-17 but had an entirely new fuselage which featured a pressurised cabin. The prototype was lost in a crash, but production aircraft were initially delivered to Pan American Airways and TWA

opposite
Vast quantities of war surplus Douglas C-47 Skytrains were flown by post-war civil operators. This military version of the DC-3 had a strengthened floor, a freight door and was powered by two 1,200 hp Pratt & Whitney Twin Wasp R radials

smoothly faired windscreen, and 40 passengers could be carried at a cruising height of 20,000 ft. The first 307 flew in December 1938, but was lost in March 1939 during flight-testing. Named Stratoliner, the 307 entered service with TWA in mid-1940, the first pressurised airliner to do so. By that time, however, air-lines were looking to the newer Lockheed and Douglas designs, and only ten production Stratoliners were built. After the Second World War, their pressurisation systems were removed, and some continued flying until the 1970s, a remarkable record indeed for so small an original fleet.

A near-contemporary of the Stratoliner was the Curtiss-Wright CW-20, also built as a larger, pres-surised replacement for the DC-3 by the company who had built the Condor biplane in the early 1930s. Powered by two of the relatively new, 18-cylinder Pratt & Whitney R-2800s, each delivering 2,000 hp, the CW-20 was flown in March 1940. By that time, however, war was looming and the airlines were not interested in a DC-3 replace-ment; the CW-20 was only saved by a USAAF order for an unpressurised freighter version under the desig-nation C-46 Commando. Some

The sole DC-4E was designed to meet the major United States airlines' request for a larger aircraft to succeed the DC-3. It was the first large transport aircraft to feature a nosewheel. Although production was planned, the DC-4E was considered too large and the only one built was sold in Japan

3,000 C-46s were built, and many were converted for airline use after the war. Although the C-46 had a higher performance and payload than the DC-3, it was never as well regarded as the Douglas type by pilots or operators.

The biggest of the immediately pre-war airliners was also the first of two aircraft "families" which were to dominate the airliner scene after the Second World War. Discussions between United Air Lines and Douglas on a new four-engined transcontinental sleeper transport had started in 1936, and in that year five US airlines (TWA, American, Pan Am, Eastern and United) agreed to share the cost of developing a prototype so as to explore the problems of such a large aircraft. The design of the DC-4, as the new prototype was known, posed new problems. Powered flying controls were introduced for the first

time, and new engine control systems had to be designed. Powered by four Pratt & Whitney R-2000s, the new aircraft was designed to carry 30 sleeper passengers or 42 day passengers (at the seating standards of the 1930s) on one-stop flights across the USA.

One of the most obvious external innovations was the nosewheel landing gear, greatly easing the ground handling and eliminating the awkward slope of the cabin floor on the ground. Eventually, the nosewheel layout was to permit reversible-pitch propellers, shortening landing runs.

Spectacular though the prototype DC-4 was, with its 138 ft wingspan and its triple tail, the airlines decided that they wanted something different. The sole example of the original DC-4 flew in June 1938, and from May the following year the fully furnished prototype was extensively tested and demonstrated by the

sponsoring airlines. The changes they recommended to the manufacturer resulted in a new aeroplane, although Douglas applied the designation DC-4 to the new aircraft as well, retrospectively naming the prototype DC-4E.

For the production DC-4, the airlines demanded pressurisation and decided to eliminate sleeper accommodation. A new, far smaller wing (spanning 20 ft less than that of the prototype) was fitted to the new aircraft, and the longitudinal stability was so much better that Douglas could revert to a single fin. The pressurised fuselage of the production aircraft was slimmer than that of the DC-4E, and of constant section for most of its length: with the exception of the Constellation, this layout was to be adopted for nearly all major airliners and was later to allow Douglas to stretch the DC-4 very easily. With its slimmer

body and smaller wing, the new DC-4 was also much faster than the prototype DC-4E. The DC-4 was ordered into production by American, Eastern and United in early 1940, but before the new aircraft flew the USA became involved in the Second World War and the DC-4 was pressed into military service. The USAAF (United States Army Air Force) C-54 Skymaster version was unpressurised, as were the 79 civil DC-4s built by Douglas after the war. In addition to those aircraft, many C-54s were converted for civil use.

Douglas, however, were not to have the market to themselves: Lockheed had designed their Model 49 in early 1939 to meet a demanding TWA specification for an airliner with the potential for non-stop transcontinental and trans-oceanic flights. The 49 was larger, more powerful and faster than the DC-4; Lockheed

Sabena were very much a Douglas airline during the monumental battle between that company and Lockheed with their Constellation. This DC-4 was pictured in 1954

One of the many Douglas DC-4s which saw service into the 1970s

decided to use the 18-cylinder Wright R-3350, nearly half as big again in capacity as the DC-4 engine and offering 2,200 hp. The wing was a scaled-up version of that fitted to Lockheed's P-38 Lightning fighter. Pressurisation was designed in from the outset. The big propellers meant a long undercarriage, and the nose of the 49 was drooped to shorten the nose-leg; the whole fuselage was cambered, reducing drag at the expense of structural simplicity and "stretchability". A triple tail was fitted, partly because the leading customer, TWA, had a hangar-height limit.

The early Model 49 designs had reverse-flow engine cowlings like those of the de Havilland Albatross (which the Lockheed aircraft resembled in some respects). However, it was eventually decided to install the engines in conventional NACA cowlings. The powerplants were installed as "power-eggs" so that all accessories and auxiliaries could be removed with the engine, greatly easing maintenance.

Compared to the DC-4, the 49 was a very high-performance aircraft, and it was partly thanks to the efficiency of the R-3350 that this was

not proportionally reflected in operating costs. In any event, Lockheed felt that the 49's higher cruising speed would force airlines to buy it in order to remain competitive; the 49 would cruise at 270 mph compared with 210 mph for the Douglas type.

Like the DC-4, the Lockheed 49 was overtaken by the Second World War. The first prototype was nevertheless completed and flown in January 1943, as the XC-69 Constellation. Only a handful of Constellations were built for the USAAF, however, in contrast to the massive number of C-54s built by 1945. However, Lockheed's position was slightly better than that of their rivals in that they had a pressurised aircraft on the production line at the end of the war. The more utilitarian DC-4/C-54 was less attractive to the airlines.

Part of the reason for the USAAF's meagre buying of Constellations, incidentally, may have been the need to conserve R-3350 production for the Boeing B-29 Superfortress, the highly sophisticated bomber that dropped the atomic weapons on Japan at the end of the war. The B-29 itself was the forebear of the

third big US piston airliner: the XC-97, a military freighter version of the B-29, made its first flight in 1944. The B-29 was a substantially heavier aircraft then either the DC-4 or the Constellation, with a high wing loading for the best possible aerodynamic efficiency. A commercial derivative of the XC-97 would thus offer better payload-range performance than its rivals, but its high wing loading made it a relatively difficult aircraft to fly and it would need a longer runway than either of its rivals. For these and other reasons, it was to be another three years before the Boeing Stratocruiser joined its Douglas and Lockheed rivals on the market.

Of all the US projects, only these three emerged in production form. The Republic company proposed the Rainbow, a development of their XR-12 strategic reconnaissance aircraft, while a Pan American requirement for a massive aircraft for wartime trans-Pacific trooping flights, and for later peacetime airline use, produced giants from Lockheed and Douglas. The two prototypes of the Lockheed R60-1 Constitution served with the US Navy, while the Douglas design, at

one time known as the DC-7, went into production as the C-74 Globemaster I and became the basis for the bigger-bodied C-124 Globemaster II freighter of the 1950s. By the end of the war, however, Pan Am and the other airlines had lost interest in such large aircraft.

At the end of the Second World War, therefore, it seemed fairly clear that the US types, chiefly the DC series and the Constellation would dominate the market for postwar airliners. Not only had conditions in the USA been far more favourable to the development of commercial-type aircraft, readily adapted to airline work, than in Britain, but only the US industry had the production capacity to meet both domestic needs (with the US airlines clamouring for new aircraft to supplement their over-stretched DC-3 fleets) and the needs of recovering foreign carriers. Granted, the British industry's output was large, but it had been built up specifically for military production, with the aid of a great deal of capacity diverted from the motor industry. Britain's heavy bombers had also been built for ease of production in small, dispersed plants rather than for

The last of the post-war Lockheed 049 Constellations to remain in service was operated by Aerovias Quisqueyana in the late 1970s

above
One of BOAC's Lockheed
Constellations (*Baltimore*) in flight

centre
Sir Arthur Whitten-Brown, left, with
Captain O. P. Jones, aboard the
flightdeck of a BOAC Lockheed
Constellation in June 1946. O. P.
Jones was one of the most
experienced airline pilots and his
career stretched from the early days
of Imperial Airways through to the
jet age with BOAC

bottom
Interior of a BOAC Lockheed
Constellation

ultimate flying performance, and they were not easy to adapt into successful airliners. The US industry had also learned a great deal during 1938–40, as the lessons of the first generation of all-metal monoplane transports were passed back to the manufacturers. The Americans had learned how to mass-produce airliners in a manner almost unknown to the British companies.

Lockheed, with a fully developed, pressurised airliner on offer, quickly took the lead. Before the outbreak of war, the US airlines had ordered 84 Lockheed 49 Constellations. The USAAF took delivery of 15 C-69s, but with the end of the war, production contracts were terminated. Lockheed found themselves with a large number of C-69s in various stages of completion, and realised that it would be mid-1947 before they could deliver a purpose-built, fully "commercialised" Constellation to any customer. However, the company decided to complete the unfinished C-69s as interim commercial aircraft, designated 049 to distinguish them from the original, pre-war 49. The first 049s were delivered in early 1946, and were used by TWA to inaugurate their first transatlantic service, between New York and Paris via Gander, (Newfoundland) and Shannon (Eire). Following the mass ferry flights of the 1939–45 war, the North Atlantic crossing had become routine for big, four-engined aircraft. Pan Am linked New York with London with the 049, and early in 1946, the British Overseas Airways Corporation, despairing of the appearance of any competitive British aircraft, also ordered the 049.

TWA soon began to operate the 049 on US transcontinental routes, taking three hours and one stop less than American Airlines' DC-4s. Douglas had realised before the end of the war that the Constellation would outclass the DC-4; nevertheless, the 049 was in service by the time the new DC-6 flew in February 1946, under the military designation XC-112A because it had been ordered in wartime by the USAAF. Compared with the DC-4, the DC-6 was externally similar, the main

difference being a 6 ft 9 in fuselage stretch. The new aircraft was, however, far more powerful, with 2,400 hp Pratt & Whitney R-2800s replacing the 1,450 hp R-2000s of the DC-4. The wing was similar in span and planform, but the trailing-edge flaps were of the new, double-slotted type, with a small slat ahead of the main flap. Together with the greater power, the new flaps allowed the DC-6 to use the same runways as its predecessor despite an increase in gross weight from 73,000 lb to 97,000 lb. Pressurisation, originally planned for the DC-4, gave the DC-6 a cruise performance comparable with that of the 049, normal cruising speeds and altitudes of the two types being roughly similar.

The DC-6 went into service in April 1947, followed in June of the same year by the Lockheed 649 Constellation and later in the year by the 749. These were the first Constellations built from the outset as airliners, and they were heavier and slightly more powerful than the 049. The 749 was a longer-range version with extra fuel in the outer wings, designed for over-water operations, while the 639 was intended for US domestic services.

Meanwhile, many of the 1,000-plus C-54s built during the war were contributing to a minor revolution in US air transport. Many had been sold as surplus to small independent airlines, who used them on ostensibly "non-scheduled", low-fare services

DC-4s were the mainstay of many European airlines in the years of post-war reconstruction: this one belonged to Air France

throughout the USA. With far higher seating densities than the scheduled carriers, they could offer substantially lower fares. The poor safety record of these airlines led to US Government moves to limit their activities to charter flights, but not before they had created a public demand for cheap air travel. The scheduled airlines responded by introducing two-class service, with denser "coach-class" seating in the front of the cabin and a first-class area at the rear (the tail being the quietest part of the piston-engined airliner, as it was farthest from the propellers). The result was that the passenger capacity of aircraft such as the DC-6 and Lockheed 649 was raised from 44 seats to over 65 seats in service; later in their lives many such aircraft were converted to seat up to 80 passengers in all-coach layouts.

In July 1947, as operations with the DC-6 and Lockheed 749 were getting under way, Boeing flew the first prototype of their Model 377, later named the Stratocruiser. Although the first XC-97 freighter had flown in 1944, it was shelved in favour of a more powerful aircraft based on the improved post-war version of the B-29 Superfortress, the B-50. The YC-97 Superfreighter was flown in late 1945, and – like the B-50 – was powered by four Pratt & Whitney R-4360 Wasp Majors. These massive 28-cylinder radials were the only four-row engines to see service; although they developed more than 3,500 hp, their sheer complexity made them unreliable and difficult to maintain.

The behaviour of the R-4360 was one of the reasons for the limited appeal of the Stratocruiser, despite the attractions of its capacious fuselage and lower-deck passenger lounge, which made it one of the most sought-after aircraft on long flights. At the time of its entry into service in 1948, it was by far the heaviest airliner in the world, grossing 145,000 lb compared with 107,000 lb for the contemporary Constellations. Its wing loading was more than 82 lb/sq ft, compared with 66 lb/sq ft for the DC-6, which accounted for its 7,200 ft take-off

above
The DC-6 was the first purpose-built version of the Douglas family, re-introducing the pressurisation which the USAAF had deleted from the DC-4

opposite
The Boeing 377 Stratocruiser was a commercial development of the military C97, which in turn grew out of the B-29 bomber. The Stratocruiser was produced at the Boeing plant in Seattle, Washington (*bottom*). The aircraft's spacious interior (*top*) was notable for its face-to-face seating and a preponderance of bare metal fittings. A good impression of the cockpit can be gained from this view (*left*) of a BOAC flight simulator

run, when the DC-6 needed only 5,400 ft. The Stratocruiser was thus limited in the number of airfields it could use.

The last of 55 Stratocruisers was delivered in March 1950, although Boeing built more than 900 C-97 and KC-97 military versions for the US Air Force. Despite this small number, the Stratocruiser did much to bolster Boeing's reputation with Pan American Airways and BOAC, both of whom made the comfortable 377 their flagship on the prestige North Atlantic route.

Between them, Douglas and Lockheed sold some 500 of the 049/649/749 series Constellations, DC-4s and original DC-6s. The fierce competition between the two US market leaders had only gone through the first round, however,

and there were to be three more rounds before the last piston airliners came off the production lines.

Only the British industry had any real chance of taking on the USA after 1945, although (for the reasons outlined earlier) it was unlikely that the British could actually have been successful. There seems to be no evidence of the often-rumoured secret agreement under which the British were said to have abdicated airliner manufacture in favour of the USA; rather, the British civil airframe industry seemed to be dogged with a certain amount of ill-luck in their efforts to close the lead which the USA, with the DC-4 and Constellation, had established in 1938–41. Pre-war projects such as the Fairey FC.2 and Short S.32 were understandably abandoned during

the early months of hostilities in favour of combat aircraft production.

Virtually the only long-range transport of British origin flying at the war's end was the Avro York, a starkly utilitarian, high-wing freighter with the wing, tailplane and Merlin engines of the Lancaster bomber. Although it performed useful service as a freighter, it was hardly a civilised airliner, even by 1945 standards.

This lack of a good airliner was partly caused by the Brabazon Committee's decision to concentrate on ambitious projects such as a jet mailplane and a massive, non-stop transatlantic airliner; the first emerged as the Comet, while the second became the Bristol 167 Brabazon. The Brabazon Committee did not recommend the development of a modern airliner for medium-to-long-haul services, but it was clear by late 1943 that such a requirement existed, and the Avro Tudor was developed as a long-range airliner, both for BOAC (which had been formed in 1940 by the merger of Imperial Airways and British Airways) and for British South American Airways (BSAA). In the same weight class

as the early DC-4s, the Tudor was pressurised, powered by four liquid-cooled Rolls-Royce Merlins and had a wing developed from that of the Lincoln bomber, a Lancaster development which had arrived too late for the war.

From the outset, two very different versions of the Tudor were envisaged: the Tudor 1, carrying just 12 passengers on transatlantic flights, and the Tudor 2 with a much longer and wider fuselage, seating as many as 60 passengers and designed for the shorter sectors of the Empire air routes. Both had tailwheel undercarriages, but were, apart from this feature, modern in conception.

The Tudor programme was nevertheless an almost unmitigated failure. Development of the transatlantic Tudor 1 took nearly two years from its first flight and it was finally rejected by BOAC in March 1946; even if the aircraft had been put into service on the North Atlantic, it could hardly have been competitive with the 40-seat Constellation, let alone the even bigger Stratocruiser which was then little more than two years away. The long-body Tudor 2, flown in March 1946, proved over-

The prototype Tudor 2, designed to carry 60 passengers over short refuelling stages on the Empire routes. This aircraft later became the prototype Tudor 7 but was destroyed in a take-off crash, killing the Avro company's chief designer, Roy Chadwick, designer of the Lancaster bomber

The Short Sandringham was more than a simple conversion of the Short S.25 Sunderland. A large number of Sunderland 5s were converted by the manufacturers at Belfast in 1945–48, re-emerging with streamlined noses and tails and with two-deck interiors including cocktail bars and accommodation for day and night passengers. This example was still being operated by Antilles Air Boats in 1979

weight and unsuitable for the many hot-and-high airfields of the African and Far East routes; it was cancelled by BOAC in 1948. Some of the cancelled Tudor 1s were completed as slightly longer Tudor 4s for BSAA but were withdrawn from passenger services after two disappeared in unexplained circumstances. Some Tudor 4s were also pressed into service on the Berlin Airlift in 1948, and Aviation Traders restored some of the type to airworthy condition in 1954 for freight

and charter work. A number of long-body Tudors also went into service, both on the Airlift and on charter work, but all were retired by 1951.

Britain's other four-engined pressurised piston airliner, the Handley Page Hermes, had an even less auspicious start to its career than the Tudor: the HP.68 prototype crashed immediately after its first take-off in December 1945. In 1947, however, BOAC ordered the stretched and improved HP.81

above
The Grumman G.73 Mallard amphibian carried ten passengers and two crew and had a cruising speed of 180 mph. Sixty-one were built between 1947 and 1951. This example, flown by Chalk's International, is seen at Miami in 1978

left
Britain's first pressurised aircraft was the Handley Page Hermes, designed during the Second World War. Because of setbacks brought about by the crash of the prototype in December 1945, the Hermes was not to enter BOAC service until 1950. The last Hermes was retired from service in 1964

Hermes 4, with four 2,100 hp Bristol Hercules radial engines and a tricycle undercarriage. These aircraft were delivered in 1950, becoming the first British aircraft of post-war design to enter BOAC service. They were used on the West African routes, but served only briefly before being replaced in 1952.

The failure of the Tudor programme necessitated the use of converted bombers on many BOAC routes. The Lancastrian, a nine-passenger version of the Lancaster, was used on a high-speed London-Australia service, while the Halton was a similarly basic conversion of the Handley Page Halifax.

Development of civil flying-boats continued in the UK after the war, culminating in the massive Saunders-Roe Princess (see next chapter). After the war, BOAC received a number of simply converted Short Sunderland patrol flying boats, known as the Hythe class, to replace the pre-war Empire boats; these were followed by the

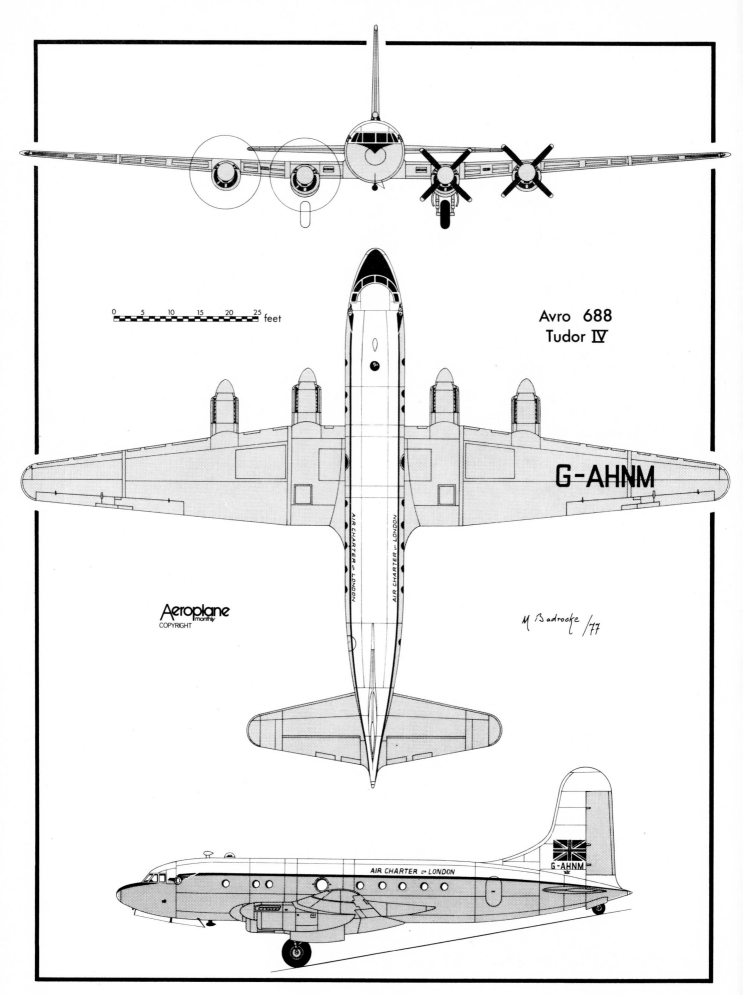

0   5   10   15   20   25 feet

Avro 688
Tudor IV

G-AHNM

AIR CHARTER LTD LONDON

AIR CHARTER LTD LONDON

Aeroplane
monthly
COPYRIGHT

M Badrocke /77

AIR CHARTER LTD LONDON

G-AHNM

above
With many structural features inherited from the Dove, the de Havilland DHA-3 Drover was produced in Australia, where it found favour with the Royal Flying Doctor Service. The rugged eight-seater could carry two pilots, two medical crew and two stretcher cases. Operating well into the 1960s, Drovers are among the few modern non-jet trimotors

left
A de Havilland D.H.114 Heron Mk2 of Ghana Airways. With seating for 14/17 passengers, the Heron (another Dove derivative) was popular as a feeder aircraft on sectors of up to 1,500 miles

opposite
Slightly more realistic than earlier versions, the Avro 688 Tudor 4 was nevertheless not a success as a rival to the US piston-engined transports

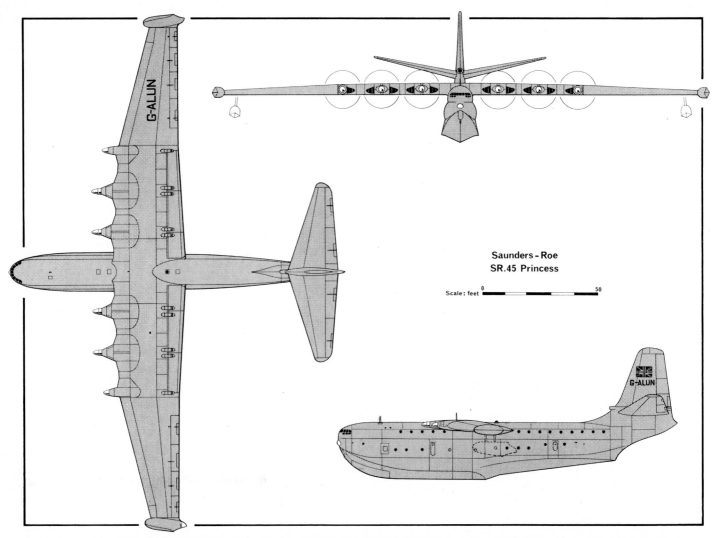

Saunders - Roe
SR.45 Princess

Scale: feet 0 ———————————— 50

Sandringham (similar to the Hythe but built as an airliner) and the Solent (developed from the Seaford, itself an improved Sunderland). The Solents actually displaced landplanes (in this case Yorks) on the route to South Africa, calling at Sicily, Cairo and Lake Victoria before alighting on a lake near Johannesburg.

The most successful four-engined airliner built outside the USA, however, was probably the Canadair C-4, a developed version of the DC-4 powered by Rolls-Royce Merlins and one of very few successful airliners to have liquid-cooled engines. Trans-Canada Airlines conceived the idea of a Merlin-powered DC-4 in 1943, and took delivery of their first Canadian-built DC-4Ms in 1947. These were followed by the pressurised DC-4M2, and in 1948, BOAC ordered the Anglicised Canadair C-4 Argonaut. Twenty-two of these aircraft were delivered to BOAC for Far East and African

routes, overcoming the political hurdle of importing aircraft directly from the United States.

In more modest ventures, however, the British industry was successful. The Bristol 170 Freighter, flown in 1945 and developed as a military transport, was not beautiful, but proved highly economical on short sectors and was suitable for operations in primitive conditions. Clamshell nose doors gave access to the capacious hold, and the Bristol Hercules engines were powerful and reliable. Extensive use of steel in the airframe meant a durable structure and low ownership costs. The Freighter was perhaps most famous in the role that it made its own – that of a vehicle-plus-passenger ferry across the English Channel. Silver City Airways' Freighters plied to and from the Continent from July 1948 until well into the 1960s, carrying travellers and their cars above the sometimes choppy waters of the English Channel at steadily de-

above
The Bristol 170 was the first British civil transport built after the Second World War. Built for low initial cost and cheap to operate, the Bristol Freighter was capable of carrying large, awkward items which could be loaded via the two hydraulically operated nose doors. This example is operated by Safe Air and is seen at Christchurch, New Zealand

opposite, top
With ten Proteus engines, the huge Saunders-Roe S.R.45 Princess was a classic example of a British design which appeared too late to have any chance of commercial success

opposite, bottom
Designed as a larger version of the Short Sunderland, the Short S.45 Solent enjoyed accident-free service with BOAC on the South Africa route, eventually being replaced with Avro Yorks. Solents carried up to 30 passengers on two decks complete with a promenade and full dining facilities

An enlarged version of the Bristol
Type 170 Freighter appeared in
1953. With its lengthened nose, the
Mk 32 was capable of carrying
three cars and saw extensive service
with Silver City Airways Ltd

creasing fares. Eventually, the
Freighters were replaced by Car-
vairs, converted from DC-4s by
Aviation Traders. Under the
guidance of Freddie Laker, Aviation
Traders fitted 747-style upper flight
decks and nose doors to the DC-4s to
allow straight-in loading of cars.

Another success, also powered by
Sir Roy Fedden's Bristol Hercules,
was the Vickers VC1 Viking. Developed from the Wellington
bomber, the Viking flew in June
1945 and became the mainstay of
British European Airways' rebuilt
European route system. Nineteen
Viking 1As with the original fabric-
covered "geodesic" wing of the
Wellington were followed by 13
Viking 1s with more conventional,
all-metal wings. The stretched 24-
seat Viking 1B followed, and over
160 Vikings were eventually built.
After their retirement from BEA,
they proved highly suited to Britain's
emerging independent airlines and
Vickers' work on the Viking laid the
foundations for its successor, the
highly successful Viscount.

above
The first post-war British transport aeroplane to enter service was the Vickers Viking. It was also the first British transport to be produced in quantity. Vikings were first flown by BEA and were to remain in airline service for 20 years

left
By converting Douglas DC-4s into car freighters, Aviation Traders Ltd provided a useful successor to the Bristol 170 Freighter. Modifications on the Carvair configuration included raising the flight deck nearly seven feet and replacing the nose with a bulbous unit allowing vehicles to be loaded via a large sideways opening door. The Carvair could carry five cars and 25 passengers

Not so fortunate was the last major British piston-engined airliner, the Airspeed Ambassador (sometimes referred to as the *Elizabethan*, its class name with BEA). One of the most refined piston-engined airliners ever developed, the Ambassador was designed to a Brabazon Committee requirement and was powered by two sleekly cowled Bristol Centaurus engines of 2,600 hp. Distinguished by its high wing and triple tail, the 47-seat Ambassador was already outclassed by the Viscount by the time it entered service in 1952. BEA, the only customer, took 20 aircraft.

France, Italy and the Soviet Union were the only other nations to emerge from the war with intact airliner industries. The French industry set to work immediately after the Liberation in 1944 to equip France's own airlines and those of her colonies. About 40 Sud-Est SE-161 Languedocs were built for Air France's European routes. The Languedoc was based on the Bloch 161, flown shortly before the outbreak of war, and was powered by four Pratt & Whitney R-1830 Twin Wasps. Despite having twice the power of the DC-3, it offered hardly any extra capacity unless four-abreast seating was fitted.

Rather more modern was the pressurised Sud-Ouest SO-30P Bretagne, used in limited numbers by some of the colonial airlines. The first prototype was completed in November 1942, but was not flown until after the Liberation. Successively enlarged versions culminated in the 37-seat production version, powered by two 2,400 hp Pratt & Whitney R-2800s.

The much larger Breguet 761 Deux-Ponts was distinguished, as its name suggests, by its two full-length passenger decks located above and below the mid-set wing. Powered by R-2800s, the production Breguet 763 could carry up to 108 passengers on both decks, or 60 on the upper deck with freight in the lower hold. First flown in 1949, a number of these aircraft were used on high-density domestic services from 1953, and some were converted to Universal freighters in the early 1960s.

Even more imposing than the Deux-Ponts was the Sud-Est SE-2010 Armagnac, at the time of its first flight the world's largest civil landplane (it was overtaken a few months later by the Brabazon). Weighing 170,000 lb for take-off, it spanned 160 ft and was powered, like the Boeing Stratocruiser, by four Pratt & Whitney R-4360 Wasp Majors. Production of 15 aircraft was started in 1949, and the last of these was to be powered by Allison T40 coupled turboprops. Like the DC-4E, however, the Armagnac's economics were penalised by the fact that it was designed with a deep fuselage for sleeper flights. Air France cancelled their order for the aircraft, finding that its economics compared poorly with those of the Constellation. Seven of the eight Armagnacs completed were put into service on a Toulouse-Saigon shuttle during the Indo-China war, after which they were withdrawn from service.

Aeroflot's standard equipment in the later war years had been the Lisunov Li-2, the Soviet-built DC-3. In 1948, the airline introduced a somewhat similar aircraft, the Ilyushin Il-12, which differed from the Li-2 in being larger and possessing a tricycle undercarriage. Powerplants were two Shvetsov ASh-82FNs, Soviet developments of the Twin Wasp, rated at 1,650 hp. The Il-12 was built in large numbers, and was superseded in 1953 by the Il-14, a somewhat larger version of the design. The Il-14M, a 36-seater version of the type, was built by Avia in Czechoslovakia and VEB in East Germany.

No post-war Soviet airliner larger than the Il-14M went into production until 1958, indicating that the development of air traffic was fettered under Stalin's regime. Two four-engined airliner prototypes were flown in the late 1940s: the Tupolev Tu-70, derived from the Boeing B-29, and the Ilyushin Il-18 (bearing no resemblance to the later turboprop Il-18) with four ASh-73s. The Tu-70 was actually developed from the Tu-4 bomber, a carbon copy of the B-29, several of which had fallen into Soviet hands following US raids on Japan.

The US industry had meanwhile not ignored the market for smaller airliners. Convair (the Consolidated-Vultee Aircraft Corporation) had made some efforts to develop a commercial freighter from the Liberator bomber; the Model 39 was demonstrated extensively, but it did not achieve commercial success, although some converted Liberators and modifications of the PB4Y-2 Privateer patrol-bomber remained in service for many years as freighters in South and Central America. Instead, the company turned their attention to an aircraft which could bring DC-6 comfort to those US routes then operated by DC-3s. The CV-110 prototype of July 1946 led to the CV-240 Convairliner; with 40 seats, the Convairliner introduced pressurisation, DC-6 speed, nose-wheel ground handling and hot meal service to shorter routes, and 176 were ordered by the airlines. (The aircraft was also built in large numbers for the US armed forces as the T-29 navigation trainer and the

C-131 transport.) Powerplants were 2,400 hp R-2800 piston engines. The stretched 240 and the heavier 440 followed in the 1950s, holding their own in most cases against the new turboprop competition.

Less success attended the US manufacturers' efforts to produce a successful "feeder-liner", an aircraft specifically designed to carry small loads of passengers on short flights into major airports. Lockheed invested several million dollars in their little, high-wing Saturn, while Boeing took their 417 to the metal mock-up stage. Douglas expended a great deal of effort developing their Super DC-3, but all the manufacturers eventually realised that the flood of war-surplus DC-3s had killed the market. Sweden's Saab 90 Scandia was another comparable aircraft, but only a handful were sold.

Martin developed their 2-0-2 in competition with the Convairliner, differing from its rival mainly in being unpressurised. A series of

above
The graceful SNCASE SE.2010 Armagnac was designed for use on the North Atlantic routes and the first production example was delivered to TAI (Transports Aériens Intercontinentaux) in April 1952. The Armagnac carried 84 first class passengers or 107 second class passengers

opposite
The most widely used Russian transport of the early 1960s was the Ilyushin Il-14. This one is seen during the opening ceremony at Moscow's Sheremetyavo Airport in 1960

structural failures forced the grounding of the type in 1948, and it did not re-enter service until 1950. Just over 100 of a redesigned and pressurised development, the 4-0-4, were sold.

Meanwhile, the full-scale battle between the Constellation and the DC-6 raged on. In 1949–50, both manufacturers announced plans to stretch their aircraft further. Douglas had already built the heavier DC-6A convertible passenger/freight aircraft for Slick Airways, while the slightly longer 82-seat DC-6B, put into service by Western Air Lines in April 1951, was a logical extension of the principle. The stretch offered a substantial improvement in the operating economics of the aircraft, and the DC-6B proved to be the most successful of the four-piston-engined Douglas family.

Lockheed, on the other hand, had more ambitious plans for the Constellation. Flight-tests with a 749 proved that the wing could lift

137,000 lb without major redesign; the L-1049 Super Constellation, flown in late 1950 and delivered to Eastern Air Lines in November 1951, weighed 120,000 lb fully loaded. The fuselage was stretched by 18 ft 4 in to seat 92 passengers, putting Lockheed well ahead in the capacity race.

However, the Super Constellation was really designed to take advantage of new powerplants: the installation of turboprops was a possibility, but none of the US engine manufacturers seemed ready to develop their engines for airline service. More available was the Wright turbo-compound engine, originally developed for long-range US Navy patrol aircraft. The turbo-compound was basically an R-3350 except that the 18 exhaust pipes were led in groups of six to three turbines connected to the crankshaft by fluid couplings. It offered 20 per cent more power for no extra fuel con-

above
The Lockheed L-1049 Super Constellation was the first stretched version of the Constellation family

opposite, top
Evolved from the experimental CV-110, the Convair CV-240 was the first of a family of medium range transports, more than 170 commercial examples being built. KLM operated a dozen 240s, many of them remaining in service for a decade

opposite, bottom
The Saab 90 Scandia was the only Swedish-built airliner to fly regular airline services. The prototype first flew in November 1946 and production aircraft were delivered to Swedish Air Lines and Aerovias Brazil. The SAS Scandias began flying on Scandinavian domestic routes in 1950 and were retired by that company in 1957

29

above
Lockheed Super Constellations under construction at the massive Lockheed Burbank plant

opposite, top
This Douglas DC-7C flew with Panair Do Brasil, a subsidiary of Pan American Airways

opposite, bottom
The prototype Lockheed Constellation was stretched 18 ft, by the insertion of two nine-foot sections, and became the prototype Super Constellation in 1951

sumption and no extra frontal area. The turbo-compound-equipped Constellation was developed on the military budget, as the US Navy's R7V-1 freighter. The extra power demanded considerable reinforcement of the wing structure. The 1049C, the first Turbo-Cyclone-powered commercial version, offered a substantial increase in speed over the transcontinental routes, and TWA placed the first order in 1950. The 1049C flew in February 1953, closely followed by Douglas' contender, the similarly engined DC-7. Both manufacturers followed with over-water developments of their new types, designated 1049G and DC-7B, but Lockheed had a 10,000 lb advantage in gross weight over the competition. Converted into range by the addition of wing-tip fuel tanks on the "Super G", these gave the Lockheed type a slight range advantage. The 1049 made the first regular non-stop transcontinental and transatlantic flights, although the latter was only possible flying from west to east. The first round in the turbo-compound battle went to Lockheed, therefore, with nearly 30 aircraft sold to the airlines plus another 320 to the USAF and US Navy. Sales of the DC-7 and DC-7B totalled 217 aircraft.

The turbo-compound engines were not received with unmixed pleasure by the passengers, although the airlines had to have them if they were to remain competitive. The high installed power made the aircraft costly to operate, as did the extra complexity of the engines. With 3,250 hp coming from each of the Wright Turbo-Cyclones on wings originally designed for barely 2,000 hp, vibration levels were high, and in the early days the engines produced long exhaust flames which sometimes disconcerted passengers on night flights.

Pan American took delivery of their first over-water DC-7Bs in the

first half of 1955, but by that time they had already ordered a new version which not only promised to alleviate some of the DC-7B's problems, but also offered – for the first time – year-round, two-way, non-stop transatlantic range. Flown in late 1955, the DC-7C *Seven Seas* went into service with Pan Am in May 1956. It introduced the first modification to the wing planform: a new centre-section increased the span by ten feet and, as well as allowing an increase in take-off weight to 143,000 lb, moved the noisy engines further away from the cabin. Fully loaded, the *Seven Seas* needed a 6,400 ft runway for take-off, 1,000 ft more than the DC-6. The engines were further developed to yield 3,400 hp, and the fuselage was stretched by another four feet.

Lockheed's counter to the DC-7C was unquestionably the ultimate piston-engined airliner, although it was without doubt less commercially successful than its Douglas rival. Unlike their rivals, Lockheed designed a completely new high-aspect-ratio wing for their L-1649A, manufactured with continuous machined skins from root to tip and built as an integral fuel tank. With a more efficient wing and greater take-off weight (156,000 lb) than the *Seven Seas*, the Lockheed aircraft offered unmatched range. The first aircraft for Lufthansa and Air France were delivered non-stop from Los Angeles, and the new aircraft, named the Starliner, operated the first trans-Polar services between London and San Francisco and between Paris and Tokyo, via Anchorage.

By the time the Starliner entered service, however, the days of the piston-engined airliner were nearly over. The Starliner lagged a year behind the DC-7C, and the lost impetus in sales was never recovered; only 43 were sold, compared with 121 *Seven Seas*. Only 18 months after the Starliner was delivered to TWA in April 1957, the first North Atlantic jet services began. Above all, however, it was the big Lockheed and Douglas airliners which, from 1945 to 1957, began to cover the globe with long-range, non-stop scheduled air services.

The DC-7 was the first Turbo-Cyclone powered version of the Douglas family, developed to counter the L-1049G Constellation

A new sound in the sky

A few days before the Luftwaffe's Heinkel He 111 bombers spearheaded the German attack on Poland, a very different aeroplane designed by the same company made its first test flight – hardly more than a hop – from Peenemünde in Northern Germany. What distinguished the little He 178 from all previous aircraft was not that it had no propeller (for numerous rocket-powered aircraft had already been tested in Germany and elsewhere) but that it was the first aeroplane to fly with a gas-turbine reaction powerplant, or turbojet.

Research into jet engines had been continuing in both Britain and Germany since the late 1920s. The Royal Aircraft Establishment at Farnborough had started experimental work aimed at producing a turbine engine for aircraft even before the Handley Page H.P.42 went into service with Imperial Airways in 1931. The RAE work, led, by Dr A. A. Griffith, brought Metropolitan-Vickers into the field of aircraft gas turbines; this firm, although they had no experience of aero-engines, had a great deal of experience in steam turbines for power generation.

A young officer cadet at RAF Cranwell, later to become Sir Frank Whittle, began work on the theory of gas turbines as an engineering thesis. He was granted a patent in 1930 and ran his first complete engine in 1937. His company, Power Jets Ltd, was responsible for the jet engine which powered the Gloster E.28/39 on the first flight of a non-German jet aircraft in May 1941. The Power Jets work was transferred that year to Rolls-Royce, combining the innovative skill of Whittle's small company with the resources of the traditionally conservative Derby manufacturer. Whittle's engines were of the "centrifugal-flow" type, in which the compressor worked by throwing air outwards through radial channels on the compressor

wheel; the German Heinkel, Junkers and BMW engines were nearly all of the more complex but much slimmer axial-flow type, now used almost universally.

Jets were so different from traditional piston engines that almost any new manufacturer had a chance to get into the market. The de Havilland Engine company, who had concentrated on smaller engines before the Second World War (rather than competing with Rolls-Royce or Bristol) began work on their own centrifugal-flow jets in 1941. The giant Wright and Pratt & Whitney companies, who had powered nearly all America's wartime combat aircraft, found themselves challenged by the US General Electric group who, with their experience of power-generating turbines and aircraft turbo superchargers, were well placed to join

the contest. Pratt & Whitney got an early start by building Rolls-Royce engines for the US Navy, and thereafter branched out on their own.

At the end of the war, however, the Americans had little interest in adopting turbines for commercial aircraft, because they were well placed to dominate the market for conventional airliners with their piston powerplants. Moreover, the poor fuel consumption of early jet engines seemed to many people to rule them out for airline use. The propeller-turbine, or turboprop, seemed a more hopeful prospect. This was essentially a jet engine in which the power was harnessed to a propeller through a reduction gear. The result was more complicated than a pure jet, but was much more efficient at speeds below 350 mph. Compared with the piston engine, the turboprop was thirstier, but it

above
Some measure of the astonishingly rapid increase in passenger air travel can be gauged from this view of London Heathrow Airport in the late 1950s. Not only were the aircraft much smaller, but there were far fewer of them then – the Queens Building at left has no aircraft at all at its bays. The public were also permitted to park their motor cars directly in front of what is now the International Terminal building

opposite
The Whittle W.1. turbojet engine first ran on April 12, 1941. It was the most refined turbojet of its time and the first Whittle to be installed in an aeroplane, its predecessors being bench test units

77

Designed as a medium stage, 26–31 seat passenger aircraft, the Armstrong Whitworth A.W.55 Apollo was a very aerodynamically clean aeroplane powered by four Armstrong Siddeley Mamba propeller turbines. The engines were unreliable, however, and the Vickers Viscount, designed to the same Brabazon Type II recommendation, won the day

promised to be lighter and slimmer. More importantly, the weight and frontal area (and thus the air resistance) of a piston engine tend to rise out of all proportion with the power, unless the number of cylinders is increased. The most powerful piston engine put into service was the 3,800 hp Pratt & Whitney Wasp Major, a 28-cylinder engineer's nightmare. Even changing the 56 spark plugs was a major operation. The turboprop offered higher power without such complexity. The US industry therefore concentrated on large turboprops of 3,000 hp and upwards (such as the Allison T38 and Pratt & Whitney T34) rather than building rivals for their own, commercially-successful, radial-piston engines.

It was left to the British to galvanise the Americans into action. Most of Britain's pre-1939 airliner programmes had been stopped in the early years of the Second World War because of the overriding need for fighters and bombers. At the end of 1941, as confidence in eventual victory grew, a committee was formed to study ways in which the lost ground could be recovered. After a year, in December 1942, this group became the Brabazon committee, under the chairmanship of pioneer aviator Lord Brabazon. With the Douglas DC-4 and the Lockheed Constellation already flying in the USA, the Brabazon Committee concluded that the only way for Britain to stay in the race was for the Government, through the Ministry of Aircraft Production, to finance development both of a number of highly advanced projects and of some more modest, interim types.

The most successful of the Brabazon Committee airliners resulted from a requirement for an

advanced airliner for use on European services, known initially as the Brabazon II. In early 1945, the Committee recommended that two types should go ahead: the Brabazon IIA (the piston-engined Ambassdor) and the IIB (a four-turboprop type). Two Brabazon IIB contenders were to be developed in parallel, with alternative engines. Armstrong Whitworth were to use the Armstrong Siddeley Mamba in their AW 55 Apollo, while Vickers decided to use the Rolls-Royce Dart for their VC2.

At that time the Dart was expected to give about 1,000 hp and the VC2 was expected to carry about 24 passengers over a 1,000-mile stage length at nearly 300 mph. It was agreed that the new aircraft would be pressurised. In April 1946, two prototypes of the new aircraft were ordered, each with 32 seats and an expected gross weight of

30,500 lb. By August 1947, the prototype design was "frozen" as the Vickers Type 630 and the choice of the Dart engine was confirmed. The earlier name – Viceroy – was dropped, as the title no longer existed after the end of British rule in India, and the new aircraft became the Vickers Viscount 630.

Success did not come easily to the Viscount. In the autumn of 1947, the newly formed British European Airways decided that the economics of the Viscount were not good enough and ordered the Ambassador (the Brabazon IIA). Work on the second Viscount 630 slowed down and construction of the third aircraft stopped altogether. The future of the Viscount still looked bleak when the prototype flew in July 1948. (It was not the first turbine transport in the air; this distinction fell to the Vickers Nene-Viking, an experimental test-bed aircraft which flew

BEA's Vickers V.701 Viscount G-AMOG photographed in 1954. A total of 27 V.701s were supplied to BEA, the first being handed over to the company in January 1953

The prototype Viscount Type 630, G-AHRF made its first flight at Wisley on July 16, 1948. For a brief period, the prototype flew on scheduled services to Edinburgh and Paris before being returning to Vickers for further development work

in April 1948.) However, it became clear that the Dart had considerable development potential beyond 1,000 equivalent horsepower (ehp) and the third Viscount prototype was reworked and stretched to become the first of the much-improved 700 series. With 1,500 ehp Dart RDa3s, the 700 was seven feet longer and had a bigger wing than the 630; with a gross weight of 45,000 lb it could seat 43 passengers. Ordered by the Ministry of Supply in February 1949, the first 700 flew in August 1950.

The fortunes of the Viscount now underwent a remarkable change. The 700 was clearly going to be a much more capable and attractive aeroplane than the Ambassador, and by 1950, BEA were once more showing interest in the turboprop. In July 1950, the first Viscount 630 made a series of highly successful proving flights on BEA's premier London-Paris route (the world's first commercial turbine flights) and these culminated in a BEA order the following month for 20 Viscount

701s, 53,000 lb aircraft with 47 seats. The production 701 flew in August 1952, two years after the prototype, and went into service with BEA in April 1953. By that time, Air France and Trans-Canada Airlines (later Air Canada) had ordered the Viscount, and Vickers had started a second production line.

Rolls-Royce, meanwhile, continued to develop the Dart and, in April 1954, BEA ordered the stretched Viscount 800 with up to 65 seats, a remarkable figure for an aircraft designed to a 24-seat specification. Also in 1954, the aircraft broke into the United States market when Washington-based Capital Airlines ordered 60 Viscount 700s. The ultimate Viscount, the 810, was a longer-range version of the 800 with a stronger structure and 1,990 ehp Dart RDa7s. Maximum take-off weight was 67,500 lb, more than twice that envisaged for the VC2 in 1946, and the 810 could carry a full, 65-passenger load for 1,500 miles at 365 mph. Before Viscount production ended in 1964,

810s had been delivered to Continental Airlines in the USA as well as to Lufthansa, South African Airways and Japan's All Nippon Airways. Of 445 Viscounts sold, 147 went to North America; the type was above all the one which made turbine engines familiar to the travelling public. It was the success of the Viscount in the USA which led to the development of the Lockheed Electra; meanwhile, proposals for further-improved Viscounts were shelved in favour of the more ambitious Vanguard, while the Viscount's rival for the Brabazon IIB specification, the Apollo was flown but abandoned in 1949.

It was one of the more ambitious Brabazon projects which resulted in the most spectacular project of the early airline age the development of the de Havilland Comet. The type, identified as Brabazon IV, was first proposed in February 1943 as "a jet-propelled mailplane for the North Atlantic," carrying no passengers but a ton of cargo. By mid-1944, the requirement had changed to an airliner for European and

Empire services, with development potential for transatlantic range, and it was this which started the innovative, idiosyncratic and technically highly successful de Havilland company thinking about a jet airliner.

The initial specification called for a 14-passenger aircraft with an 800-mile range, but by late 1944, when the British Overseas Airways Corporation indicated that they would need 25 Brabazon IV types,

de Havilland were thinking about a 24-seater with four of their own, 5,000 lb-thrust Halford H2 centrifugal-flow turbojets (later known as the de Havilland Ghost). Throughout 1945, de Havilland's chief designer, Ronald Bishop and his team worked in considerable secrecy on the D.H.106 project, a radical, tail-less design with a 40° swept wing. In early 1946, however, de Havilland decided that the tail-less layout was too dangerous for an

above
The Viscount, seen in the colours of its major operator, British Airways

opposite, top
The fastest ever Vickers Viking was the Nene powered variant, which held the honour of being the first British pure jet transport

opposite, bottom
One of the very few British aircraft to sell in bulk to foreign carriers, the Vickers Viscount was even operated by Lufthansa

airliner (all three examples of the D.H.108, originally built to test such a configuration for the airliner, having been destroyed in fatal accidents) and added a tailplane.

In September 1946, the Ministry of Supply confirmed an order for two prototypes of the D.H.106, and late that year, Bishop's team reached what was virtually the prototype-standard design, reducing the sweep of the wings from 40° to 20°, trading speed for payload while also avoiding some of the more severe stability problems of sharply swept wings. By this time, the design was a 32-

passenger aircraft, by the generous seating standards accepted on international routes at the time. Towards the end of 1947, the name Comet was adopted, but development continued to be shrouded in secrecy and the existence of the aircraft was not officially revealed until April 1949, less than four months before it first flew.

The Comet's maiden flight in July 1949 caused a sensation in Britain and something like panic in the USA. Its cruising speed of just over 500 mph clearly represented unbeatable competition for the slow, piston-engined airliners – and the 2,000-mile range Comet 1 was only the beginning: since late 1946, de Havilland had been looking at improved versions of the Comet with the axial-flow Rolls-Royce AJ.65 and enought range to fly the Atlantic with one stop.

The Comet 1 was a 36/44-seat aircraft weighing 105,000 lb for take-off, of which some 40,000 lb was fuel, carried in "integral" wing tanks: that is to say, the wing itself was sealed to act as a fuel tank. The aerodynamics were conventional, unlike the structure, which made extensive use of metal-to-metal bonding istead of riveting. In order to exploit the characteristics of the jet, the Comet was designed to cruise at altitudes up to 40,000 ft, above all but the worst tropical storms; this called for a far greater degree of cabin pressurisation than had been used before. All the flying controls were power-operated.

Flight tests of the two Comet prototypes proceeded well, and the white-topped jets left a trail of shattered point-to-point speed records wherever they went. The only major change between the prototypes and the first production aircraft, flown in January 1951 and delivered to BOAC in early 1952, was a switch from single-wheel main undercarriage units to four-wheel bogies. Air France, UAT (the other main French international carrier, later UTA) and Canadian Pacific Airways (now CP Air) followed BOAC on to the Comet 1 order book.

By the time the Ghost-powered Comet 1 entered service in May

1952, operating the world's first regular jet service from London to Johannesburg, the forthcoming Avon-powered version was seen as the definitive aircraft. The first Avon-powered Comet, the 2X flew in February 1952, and the production Comet 2 promised better range and a higher payload resulting from a longer fuselage, better fuel consumption from the axial jets and a higher take-off weight.

In September 1952, de Havilland announced the Comet 3, with a further stretched fuselage to seat 58/76 passengers, 9,000 lb-thrust Avon RA.26s and 145,000 lb gross weight. This was the transatlantic Comet, whose 2,700-mile range was adequate for one-stop crossings. The Ministry of Supply ordered a prototype Comet 3, and orders were placed by BOAC and Air-India. Then, in October 1953, Pan American Airways ordered three Comet 3s and took "options" (paid-up reserved delivery) on seven more. With production already under way at Hatfield (the home of de Havilland) and starting at Shorts in Belfast, and with the prospect of a third assembly line at Chester, the Comet seemed set to dominate the

airline industry. The Comet 3 was due to fly in 1954 and enter service in 1956, two years ahead of any conceivable US competitor.

By late 1953, however, all was not well with the Comet programme: the first Comet loss had occurred five months after services started, when one of BOAC's Comet 1s failed to become airborne during a night take-off from Rome. Nobody was injured, but the pilot was blamed for the incident and demoted from the Comet fleet to flying York freighters. Then, in March 1953, Canadian Pacific's first Comet was destroyed in a similar accident at Karachi on its delivery flight, with the loss of 14 lives. These accidents occurred because the Comet 1 had a rather tricky take-off characteristic: if the nose was pulled up too sharply, the wing could stall while the aircraft was still on the ground. The problem was compounded by the rather coarse artificial "feel" built into the Comet's power controls, which were much less sensitive than modern systems and at night it was all too easy to misjudge the take-off angle. The Comet wing leading-edge was later modified to alleviate the problem; later still, the captain of the

A sight that was never seen on the world's airways, a Comet modelled in Pan American colours to mark the US airline's provisional order for the type. By the time the Comet had overcome its initial problems, however, the Boeing 707 had flown and Pam Am no longer needed to buy British

above
A selection of Comet variants undergoing routine maintenance in the BOAC hangar at London Heathrow Airport

right
The prototype de Havilland D.H.106 Comet, G-ALVG, made its first flight from the company aerodrome at Hatfield on July 27, 1949. The 31 minute flight was made by chief test pilot John Cunningham and a crew of four

aircraft wrecked at Rome was exonerated. Present-day civil aircraft have to demonstrate that they can take-off with the lowest point of the rear fuselage actually scraping the ground.

By the beginning of 1954, BOAC's Comet 1s had each accumulated up to 3,000 hours in the air. On January 10, Comet G-ALYP, which had operated the airline's first service, broke up in flight near Elba in clear weather, following a take-off from Rome. The Royal Navy was called in to recover the wreckage for investigation, and the Comet fleet was grounded and minutely inspected. Although no outside cause for the Elba crash could be found, it was equally true that no fault had been found with the Comet itself, and the theory that the crash was due to sabotage became widely accepted. On March 23, therefore, the Comets were put back into service; on April 8, another BOAC Comet broke up in flight, this time off Naples; the fleet was grounded again.

Salvage efforts off Elba were now intensified, and eventually some 75 per cent of G-ALYP's airframe was fished from the Mediterranean and pieced together at the Royal Aircraft Establishment at Farnborough. One Comet was taken from the BOAC fleet and installed in a static test rig, where hydraulic jacks simulated flight loads on the airframe. The

This de Havilland Comet 1, G-ALYP, was delivered to BOAC in March 1952 and crashed into the sea off Elba in January 1954. Similar accidents to other Comet 1s resulted in the type being withdrawn from service. The cause of the crashes was eventually traced to explosive decompression of the pressure cabins and the Comet 1 was withdrawn permanently

fuselage was immersed in water and the water pressure inside the fuselage was varied to simulate changes in pressurisation loads with climb and descent. (Water, rather than air, was used because the effects are far less destructive when a failure does occur.)

The test fuselage failed after 1,800 "flights", and it was found that the loadings around windows and other cut-outs in the hull were higher than anyone had suspected. The Court of Inquiry, convened in October 1954, concluded that nobody was to blame for the accidents: de Havilland and BOAC had simply pushed too far into the unknown.

Meanwhile, the Comet 3 prototype flew in July 1954, but this was now only a development aircraft for the Comet 4, modified to incorporate

the lessons of the Comet 1 crashes. By this time, the Boeing 707 was under development and the race was on between Pan Am and BOAC to operate the first truly transatlantic jet service. The Comet 4 flew in April 1958 and went into service on the London-New York route on October 4 of that year, 22 days ahead of Pan Am's 707-120s. But the intercontinental versions of the 707 and DC-8 were now under development, with non-stop transatlantic range. The writing was on the wall for the Comet.

Later versions of the Comet included the 4B, stretched to carry 102 passengers but less fuel and with a shorter wing than the standard 4. The 4C, sold to operators who needed the hot-and-high airfield performance which the early Ameri-

left
The wireless communication and navigation equipment on a Comet, with the instrument landing system at the top

left, bottom
The pantry of an early BOAC Comet 4 — a far cry from the comprehensive facilities provided on a modern jet

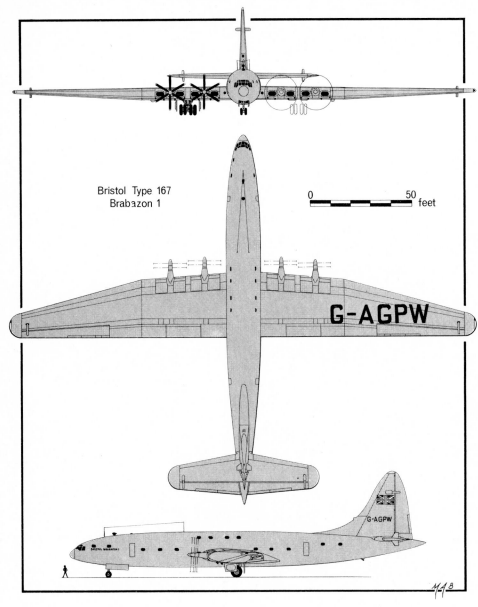

Bristol Type 167
Brabazon 1

0   50 feet

G-AGPW

G-AGPW

can jets lacked, combined the stretched fuselage with the standard wing, but the Comet was never really a competitor in the big-jet sales boom of the late 1950s, and production ended in 1962.

The immediate post-war years saw the development in the UK of two outsize, long-haul airliners, one designed to a Brabazon Committee specification. The first to fly, in September 1949, was the Bristol 167, designed to the Brabazon I specification for a non-stop transatlantic airliner to carry 80 passengers with sleeper accommodation. It was actually named the Brabazon, after the Committee's chairman. The first aircraft – the only example flown – had eight Bristol Centaurus radial piston engines, but the second and subsequent aircraft would have had Proteus turboprops from the same

manufacturer. The engines were buried within the thick wing in pairs, driving contra-rotating airscrews. Impressive as the 300,000 lb, 230 ft-span Brabazon was, it was too large for the technology of its day; smaller, four-engined types could do the same job more economically. It was also apparent that the thick wing with buried engines was not the best design solution (it responded badly to turbulence), while the coupled propellers also gave trouble; this caused the abandonment of a BEA plan to operate the prototype, with 180 seats, on London-Nice holiday flights.

The other giant, with ten Proteus, was the Saunders-Roe Princess flying-boat. Flown in August 1952, the Princess remained under development for four years, despite the fact that BOAC had discontinued their flying-boat operations in 1950. One prototype was flown, and the airframes of two others were completed, but all three remained wrapped in anti-corrosive sheeting at Cowes until the mid-1960s, the subject of various proposals to convert them into outsize landplane freighters or even fitting them with airborne nuclear powerplant, before they were broken up.

One of the two, long-haul turbo-prop airliners built in quantity was a British design developed outside the Brabazon Committee projects. The Bristol 175 Britannia originated from a BOAC specification issued at the end of 1946 for a "Medium-Range Empire" transport. Bristol's first proposal was to build the Lockheed Constellation under licence with their own Centaurus engines, but this solution was rejected because of the high cost in scarce US dollars. Bristol responded with a home-grown, 103,000 lb airliner capable of carrying up to 48 passengers from Johannesburg to Nairobi, for service from 1954. In July 1948, the Ministry of Supply ordered three, Centaurus-powered Type 175s, with the provision that at least two of them could be fitted with Proteus turbo-props if the new engine's promise was realised. The new design tended to grow during development, particularly as BOAC decided to meet

above
Typical of the high lift devices fitted
to the airliners of the late 1940s and
early 1950s were the powerful
double-slotted flaps of this Bristol
Britannia

right
Eight of the first nine production
Bristol Britannia turboprop aircraft
in course of final assembly at Filton

the lower end of their "Medium-Range Empire" requirement with the Canadair C-4 Argonaut. In July 1949, Bristol began studies of a 130,000 lb version of the 175, suitable for non-stop transatlantic services; by the following year, the 175 had definitely outgrown the Centaurus, and the Proteus was chosen as the standard engine.

The first Britannia flew in August 1952, and its relative quietness compared with piston-engined airliners won it the popular name of "Whispering Giant." By this time it was a 90-seater, tipping the scales at 140,000 lb for take-off, with double-slotted flaps over nearly two-thirds of the wingspan. Unfortunately, the Proteus had other attributes which were less advantageous than its low noise level. The second prototype was written off only weeks after its first flight, when it force-landed on

the River Severn mudflats following an engine fire. Proving flights on BOAC's African and Eastern network started in September 1954, but the engine was not brought to an acceptable level of reliability until the end of 1956. By the time the medium-range Britannia 100 entered service in February 1957, the type had missed its chance on world markets. The production Britannia 100 weighed 155,000 lb at take-off and, with four 3,780 ehp Proteus 705s, could carry 90 passengers about 2,400 miles. The stretched, transatlantic Britannia 300 series followed quickly after the 100, but arrived on the North Atlantic (with BOAC and El Al) only ten months before the first jet operations started. With more powerful Proteus engines, rated at up to 4,500 ehp, and weighing up to 185,000 lb, BOAC's Britannia 300 carried up to 114

The Bristol Type 175 Britannia was designed for use on BOAC's Empire routes. The Proteus 625 powered prototype first flew on August 16 and Britannias entered service with BOAC on February 1, 1957, the world's first long-range propeller turbine transport to do so

above
The world's first long-range
propeller-turbine powered transport
aircraft to enter service was the
Bristol Type 175 Britannia. Main
operators of the type were BOAC,
but the Corporation sold off many
of their aircraft to independent
airlines, including British Eagle

opposite
Two generations of British
passenger aircraft seen at Gatwick
Airport: a Dan Air Comet is seen
beyond the engines of a Britannia

passengers in conditions well
removed from the noise and
vibration of the last piston giants, but
the engine problems and delays
condemned it and the hoped-for
US sales did not materialise.

It was natural that Bristol should
consider alternative powerplants for
the Britannia and, in the mid-1950s,
the company were convinced that
the long range and low fuel consumption of the turboprop would
beat the pure jet on longer routes.
Bristol's own, 5,500 ehp Orion turboprop was flight-tested in a Britannia,
and the company studied a 500 mph
development of the type, with a
thin wing and two passenger decks,
under the designation Bristol 187.
But the British Government cancelled Orion development in favour
of the Rolls-Royce Tyne in 1958, and
by the end of that year it was clear
that there was no substitute for jet
speed. The Britannia lines at Filton
and Belfast (where the type had been
built for the RAF) closed in 1960,
after 83 aircraft had been built, but
the Britannia story was not quite
over: Shorts used the Britannia wing,

with Tynes, for their Belfast military
freighter, while Canadair obtained a
licence to build Tyne-powered
Britannias under the designation
CC-106 Yukon for the Royal
Canadian Air Force. Further
Canadair developments of the type
included the piston-engined CL-28
Argus maritime aircraft and the
swing-tail CL-44D civil freighter,
sold to a number of US freight airlines. The last of the line was the
stretched, 189-seat CL-44J built for
the Icelandic carrier Loftleidir, who
needed an aircraft to operate cheap,
scheduled transatlantic flights.

While the British pioneered turbine transport with the short-haul
Viscount, the medium-haul Comet
and the intercontinental Britannia,
the rest of the world followed
cautiously behind. One exception to
this rule was Canada, where Avro
Canada flew their C-102 Jetliner
with four Rolls-Royce Nenes only
months after the first Comet had
taken to the air. A less adventurous
design than the Comet, it was
correspondingly less efficient and
less attractive, and its straight wing

offered too small a speed advantage over the conventional airliners to be worthwhile. The first US turbine transport flew in 1950: a Convair CV-240, re-engined with Allison T38s. The US Air Force tested a small assault transport with four General Electric J47s, the Chase XC-123A. Not surprisingly the result was a mismatch, although the piston-engined C-123B (the Fairchild Provider) later proved successful as a military transport. The US Air Force and Navy fitted the big, Pratt & Whitney T34 turboprop to a few Boeing C-97s (the military version of the Stratocruiser) and to Lockheed C-121s (military Constellations) for extensive proving trials, but the conservative US airline industry preferred to stick to

their piston engines. The Douglas DC-7D, proposed in 1955 as a Tyne-powered version of the DC-7C *Seven Seas*, similarly failed to attract interest. With the exception of Boeing, who in any case were looking at a military market for their Model 367–80 (the prototype 707/717 jet transport/tanker), the USA seemed to be wishing that the gas turbine would go away.

France, by contrast, saw her aircraft industry as a symbol of post-war resurgence and was very keen to build her own jet airliner. Like the British Government, the French Government decided to fit jets on a standard airliner to acquire operational experience; the resulting Sud-Ouest SO-30R flew in March 1951. At about the same time, the

above
Similar in appearance to Britain's Avro Tudor 8 was the Canadian Avro C-102 Jetliner, first flown in August 1949. The first flight ended with undercarriage failure and a subsequent belly-landing

opposite, top
Deliveries of the Canadair Forty Four (CE-44), the world's first swing-tail long-range transport, began in June 1961

opposite, bottom
Construction of the C-102 Jetliner under way at A V Roe (Canada) Limited in 1948. The first prototype crashed and work on the second aircraft was stopped. The design never went into production, being outclassed by both the Comet and the Boeing 707

97

Pictured here, the prototype Sud Caravelle VI-R is painted in United livery, although this actual aircraft was sold to Cruzeiro de Sol

Sud-Est division of France's nationalised airframe industry, based at Toulouse, started talking to Air France about a possible jet airliner to serve that carrier's European network. The French Government organised a design competition within the French industry, which was won by the SE-210, later named Caravelle, in February 1953.

Designed by Pierre Satre, the Caravelle was a design of revolutionary genius. Its most striking feature was the location of the two Rolls-Royce Avon RA.29 engines – basically similar to those developed for the Comet 2 and 3 – on the sides of the rear fuselage, below a mid-height tailplane. This kept the high-velocity exhaust of the pure jet away from the structure, and the jet noise away from the cabin. It also permitted a clean, uncluttered wing; Satre chose a 20° swept wing, like that of the Comet, but with a considerably higher aspect ratio giving lower drag, particularly in the climb. With area-increasing flaps arrayed along 58 per cent of the span, the Caravelle could take off at two-thirds the weight of a Comet 4 on little more than half the power. The achievement of the French team was even more surprising when one considers that take-off performance for certification has to be demonstrated with one engine failed, in which case the Caravelle had only a third of the Comet's power at its disposal. A further advantage of the rear engine installation is that the asymmetric-thrust problems of flying with one engine out are reduced to a minimum.

The Caravelle flew from Toulouse in May 1955 and entered service with Air France four years later. Unusual features included the built-in air-stair under the tail, the sailplane-type "fence" airbrakes in the wing and the use of a braking parachute for landing. In 1959, United Airlines surprised everyone by ordering 20 Caravelle VIs, with thrust reversers and other changes. Sud-Est discussed the possibility of licensing the Caravelle design to Boeing and later Douglas, who were both understandably worried by the United order, but both US manufacturers preferred to develop their own aircraft in the hope that the Caravelle would not make further inroads into the US market before the new US

The Caravelle sold extensively within Europe, this original Caravelle VI being operated by Spanish flag carrier Iberia

The Tupolev Tu-104 was the
second jet airliner to go into service.
It retained the glazed nose of its
military ancestor, the Tu-16
bomber

jets were ready. In the event, the US
manufacturers were right, partly
because the French failed to re-
inforce their success early enough.
This in turn was partly due to
uncertainty as to whether the Caravelle was to be built in the USA, and
to an abortive sales agreement
reached with Douglas. A stretched
Caravelle, the Super A with aft-fan
General Electric CJ805-23Bs, was
flown in April 1962, but by that time
the Boeing 727 and BAC One-Eleven
were under full-scale development
and the DC-9 was near to a go-ahead.
A few Caravelle 10s and 12s were
built in the late 1960s, with JT8D
engines, bringing production to a
close. Despite the lack of development put into the Caravelle, it
remained Europe's best-selling jet at
the time of writing, with a total of
280 sales.

Next in the medium-jet stakes was
the Soviet Union, which used a

diplomatic visit to London in 1956
as the opportunity to reveal its new
Tupolev Tu-104 Camel to a surprised world. The Camel had flown
in the previous year, and was plainly
a simple adaptation of the Soviet Air
Force's standard medium jet
bomber, the Tu-16 Badger. The
Tu-104 used the Tu-16 wing virtually unchanged, and even retained
the bomber's glazed nose (navi-
gational facilities were perhaps not
all that they might have been within
the Soviet Union!) Many of the
Tu-104's features were repeated on
later Tupolev transports. The landing gear retracted rearwards into
large pods on the trailing edge of the
wing (a layout later evaluated by
Boeing for the 727) rather than
retracting inwards in accordance
with Western practice. The wing was
highly swept, but lacked any leading-
edge devices and carried fairly
simple Fowler flaps. Landing speeds

of the early Soviet jet airliners thus tended to be high. The most striking feature, however, was the use – in an aircraft the size of the Comet – of two, vast 20,000 lb-thrust turbojet engines (Mikulin AM-3s in the early Tu-104 and Tu-104A, and Mikulin RD-3Ms in the stretched Tu-104B, the main production version). These were, however, somewhat crude powerplants, and the aircraft did not compare well with the contemporary Comet 4; weighing slightly more than the British aircraft, at 167,000 lb, the Tu-104B carried the same number of passengers only about 60 per cent as far. The first Tu-104s went into service in September 1956 and the Tu-104B followed in April 1959. A four-engined version, the Tu-110 (with four, 11,000 lb-thrust AL-5s) was flown in 1959 but not proceeded with; over 160 Tu-104s were eventually built.

A purely experimental transport of the late 1950s was the East German VEB 152, which possessed the distinction of being the first German jet aircraft since 1945. It was a highly unusual design, with four engines in two twin pods, a high-swept wing and a "bicycle" under-carriage. The first prototype crashed on an early flight; a second, designated the 152-II, was modified and flown, but the programme was abandoned in 1960.

Rather more success attended a group of closely similar aircraft which emerged during the second half of the 1950s to meet an antici-pated need for a DC-3 replacement. The term was something of a mis-nomer, as most of the DC-3s in service had been bought as war-surplus and their operators could never hope to replace them with a new type straight off the production line. All the successful Western con-

Fairchild Industries produced a long-fuselage development of the F-27 Friendship, the first of which made its maiden flight in April 1958. Many variants of the FH-227 were built and the FH-227E could seat 44–52 passengers. When production ceased, a total of 201 had been built

tenders in the market used the tried and proven Rolls-Royce Dart turbo-prop, which continued to increase in output year by year. First on the scene were the Dutch Fokker company, who decided that the elusive DC-3 replacement was an ideal first post-war civil project for their reconstructed organisation. Studies started in 1950, and the Netherlands Government financed the development of two prototypes in September 1953. The first F.27 Friendship flew in 1955, the Irish airline Aer Lingus being the first carrier to order the type. Fokker reached an agreement with Fairchild under which the American company would build Friendships in the USA; the first US-manufactured aircraft flew in April 1958, and a US operator was the first to put the type into service in September of that year. Aer Lingus put the first Dutch aircraft into service in December 1958, and the type went on to become the best-selling European airliner, with well over 600 units sold.

The second of the twin-Dart air-liners to fly was the Handley Page HPR7 Herald, in March 1958. In fact, the airframe had flown in August 1955, with four Alvis Leonides piston engines, but the company realised (with the advent of the Friendship) that the market was prepared to make the jump to gas-turbine power. The Herald went into service in May 1961, but did not sell widely outside the United Kingdom. Handley Page were also badly affected by a British Government ruling that no military or government contracts could be given to firms who did not fall into line with their plans for the reorganisation of the British aircraft industry, and the Herald went out of production in 1968, after 48 aircraft had been completed.

The third of the group to appear was the Avro 748 (later the Hawker Siddeley 748 and finally the British Aerospace 748). Unlike the Friend-ship and Herald, it was a low-wing design, bringing lower drag and a shorter, lighter undercarriage, but complicating its use in the cargo role. More than 300 748s have been

opposite, top
The Sud-Aviation SE-210 Caravelle VI-R was similar to the VI-N but had a modified windscreen to give better visibility. The VI-R was powered by two Avon 532R or 533R turbojet engines fitted with thrust reversers. This Austrian Air Lines example is leaving Heathrow

opposite, bottom
One of the prototype Handley Page Dart Heralds in BEA colours during its early proving operations in Scotland

below
The F.27 was always popular with the smaller airlines, especially those operating in difficult areas. These New Zealand National examples are seen at Wellington in 1974

above
Similar in appearance to the
H.S.748 was the Japanese NAMC
YS-11 twin-turboprop short/
medium range transport; first flown
in August 1962, it remained in
production until 1971

right
Design of the Hawker Siddeley
(originally Avro) H.S. 748 began in
1959 and the prototype flew a year
later. Illustrated here is a Mount
Cook Airlines 748 flying beside
Mount Aspiring in New Zealand

sold, however, making it second only
to the F.27 among current European
airliners.

All three European types were
broadly similar, with about 40 seats
in their original versions, gross
weights in the 40,000 lb bracket and
wing areas around 800 sq ft. The
Herald was slightly heavier than the
other two and used slightly more
powerful Darts, corresponding to
later versions of the Avro and the
Fokker.

The fourth twin-Dart to appear,
however, was rather different: the
NAMC YS-11 was built by the
Nihon Aeroplane Manufacturing
Company, a consortium of Japanese
manufacturers including Mitsubishi,
Kawasaki and Showa. Designed for
a specific Japanese requirement, it
ran two years behind the 748, the
last of the European twins to appear,
and used the 3,050 ehp Dart RDa10
rather than the 2,150 ehp variants
used by the Europeans. Its wing was
bigger and carried double-slotted
flaps and, like the 748, it was a low-
wing design. Weighing just over
50,000 lb, it was designed to carry
60 passengers over short stage
lengths. Namco had some success
in selling the YS-11 to US operators,
prompting Fairchild to build a

above
Intended as a DC-3 replacement, the 28-seat Aviation Traders A.T.L.90 Accountant 1 was powered by two 1,740 hp Rolls-Royce Dart 512 turboprops. One aircraft only was built in 1957 and the project was abandoned

right
The Antonov An-24 was designed to operate from small airfields on Aeroflot's feeder-line routes; it entered service in 1963

opposite, *above*
One of several twin-RR Dart-engined airliners to appear in the late 1950s, the Handley Page Herald was not a commercial success, only 48 being made

opposite, *bottom*
The Armstrong Whitworth A.W.65 Argosy, later known as the Hawker Siddeley H.S.650 Argosy, was a medium range, twin boom freighter with a podded fuselage designed as a general purpose transport. A total of 56 Argosy C.Mk 1s were built for the RAF and 18 Argosy Series 101, 102 and 222 aircraft were supplied to civilian operators

stretched F.27, designated FH-227, in defence. Perhaps surprisingly, the US industry did not come up with its own aircraft in the category, although many Convair 340s and 440s were converted to take Allison 501s or Darts.

Mention must also be made of the British Aviation Traders Accountant, an interesting attempt by Freddie Laker's Aviation Traders engineering company to break into the aircraft manufacturing market. The Accountant used Napier Elands rather than Darts and embodied some innovative structural ideas, but it was not successful.

The Soviet Antonov bureau produced Aeroflot's equivalent of the Friendship, the An-24 Coke, which sired a family of civil and military aircraft, some versions of which added a booster turbojet to the two Ivchenko AI-24 turboprops.

One of the last products of the Dart era was the Hawker Siddeley Argosy, a twin-tailboom specialised freighter with four Darts. As many have found since, the market for a specialised civil freighter is not large; most of the Argosies built were delivered to the Royal Air Force.

These, then, were the aircraft that got the turbine age well under way in Europe in the 1950s. American technology had not been idle, however, as the next chapter will show.

Jet set

The first flight of the Lockheed Constellation in 1943 marked the start of a 12-year period during which the United States produced not one large new airliner, despite the fact that technology was advancing as never before. Development of both the Constellation and the Douglas DC-7, and of their Wright piston engines, continued right up to 1957.

The initiative that produced the first US jet airliner came from the company which had least to lose if the piston airliners became obsolete. Boeing had enjoyed only a limited success with their Stratocruiser, although they built a large fleet of tanker/transport versions for the US Air Force; similarly, Pratt & Whitney found that the commercial engine market, at least in the larger sizes, was dominated by Wright.

Both companies thus had the incentive and the technology to start a new generation of jet transports. In May 1945, a Boeing team led by the company's chief aerodynamicist, George Schairer, took part in the massive investigation of German aviation technology which followed the end of the Second World War in Europe. They found a vast amount of advanced, theoretical work on the use of sharply-swept wings to allow speeds of the order of 90 per cent of that of sound. The theory of swept wings had been advanced in a paper read to a Rome conference in 1935, but it had been ignored outside Germany. At the Junkers design office, Schairer and his team made an even more significant discovery: an advanced design study for a swept-wing jet bomber designated EF 150. The design was remarkable,

with a tandem-wheel undercarriage, drooping, high-set wings and a T-tail. The most revolutionary feature, however, was the mounting of the engines, which were carried ahead of and below the wings on slim, fragile-looking pylons. It looked eccentric, but Boeing soon realised that it worked. The US company were designing a jet bomber for a US Army Air Force competition and the engine installation was giving trouble. If the engines were attached directly to the wing, as on a piston-engined aircraft, they created shock waves as soon as the aircraft got to 70 per cent of the speed of sound. At the time of the German surrender, Boeing were trying, without much success, to convince the USAAF that engines buried in the fuselage would not be an unacceptable fire hazard. But pylon mountings carried the

108

engines well ahead of the wing and eliminated the shock wave. Moreover, the weight of the engines hung on the wing served to spread the total weight along the span, reducing bending loads and permitting a significantly lighter wing structure.

Ironically, the designer of the Junkers EF 150, Professor Brunolf Baade, found himself in the Russian sector after the fall of Germany. The EF 150 was eventually built and flown in Russia, and Baade went on to build the VEB 152 airliner in East Germany.

Boeing, meanwhile, wasted no time in redesigning their Model 450 submission to the USAAF competition along the German lines, albeit with six engines instead of two. The result was an order for two prototype XB-47s, but no production order; the USAAF was not quite convinced that the Boeing aircraft, with its 35° swept wing and podded engines, would work, and ordered a number of straight-wing bomber prototypes as well.

The XB-47 Stratojet flew in October 1947, but the USAAF still doubted whether the jet had enough range for a strategic bombing role. Finally, Boeing persuaded the USAF (as it was renamed in 1948) that the B-47 could do the job with the aid of airborne tankers, external fuel tanks and rocket-assisted take-off, and they won an order for a much bigger eight-jet intercontinental bomber, the B-52.

above
Biggest Boeing jet before the 367-80 was the eight-engined, 185 ft-span B-52 Stratofortress. The first 707s were powered by civil versions of the Pratt & Whitney J57s developed for the B-52

opposite
First aircraft to fly with the pylon-mounted engines of the Boeing 707 was the same company's B-47 Stratojet bomber. The tail parachute was not generally considered suitable for airline use, although it was used on early Caravelles

109

By this time, Boeing could reasonably claim to be pre-eminent in the design of large transonic aircraft, and (not surprisingly) the company's thoughts turned to the idea of a comeback on the airliner scene. In 1947 and 1948 the company studied aircraft looking much like the B-47, with high wings and tandem wheels. There was increasing concern in the US industry about the Comet, the existence of which was being rumoured at the time. There was even an attempt in the US Congress to arrange government funding for a jet airliner, as none of the US airlines seemed interested in putting up the necessary development costs, but this came to nothing.

The B-47 layout was still far from suitable for an airliner, as Boeing quickly realised: the Stratojet's wing was "dry" with no integral tanks, which meant that the fuel had to be carried in the fuselage; the aircraft also had a very high landing speed and was tricky to fly. The bicycle undercarriage did not make for easy ground handling and the main spar box of the high wing would have interrupted the passenger cabin. In October 1949, Boeing produced a configuration which looked something like the modern 707, with four jet engines in separate pods and a conventional undercarriage retracting inwards into a low-set wing, with the main spar box passing beneath the cabin floor.

The Boeing B-52 programme was also producing a powerful, reliable powerplant for any new airliner, in the shape of the Pratt & Whitney J57. This was the first American two-spool engine, more powerful and more efficient than earlier designs.

In June 1950, the "Cold War" flared up in Korea, and Boeing found themselves fully occupied with military contracts. But with the large fleets of jet bombers coming into service, Boeing saw a growing need for a jet-powered tanker to replace the KC-97 Stratocruisers they were building at the time. In August 1951, the company suggested to the US Air Force that the KC-97 should form the basis of a jet transport/tanker, with J57s in paired pods under a new swept wing. The proposal was rejected, but Boeing felt certain that the B-47s and B-52s would eventually need a jet tanker, and continued to study variations on the KC-97 (which carried the company designation Model 367). As studies progressed, the company came back to the all-new design of 1949, and started concentrating on an aircraft which could be developed both into a tanker for the USAF and into a commercial airliner. In April 1952, Boeing decided to risk several million dollars on the construction of a prototype jet transport tanker, rather bigger than the Comet 3, which was announced in the same year. The prototype was designated the 367-80, although it bore no relation to the KC-97 and the company had already decided that production airliners would be called 707s.

Boeing's first efforts were directed towards obtaining a USAF order for the Model 717, the standard tanker version of the 367-80. The prototype was rolled out in May 1954, but was severely damaged during taxiing trials when a faulty undercarriage forging broke. It was hardly a good omen. The 367-80 finally flew in July 1954; known as the "Dash 80", that first prototype was destined for a long and infinitely varied flight-testing career, during which it tested virtually every feature of the subsequent Boeing transports and many ideas which the company discarded. Eventually, in 1972, the "Dash 80" was honourably pensioned off to the US National Air & Space Museum. But in 1954, Boeing's US competitors – particularly the established airliner manufacturers – watched the 367-80 with interest and waited for Boeing to lose their money. Douglas had shown a DC-8 mock-up to the airlines in 1952, but after a considerable amount of work had announced at the end of 1953 that they were suspending research into jet airliners. Like Lockheed, they were concentrating on non-stop intercontinental versions of their established, piston-engined types. When the 367-80 flew in 1954, more than two years after the decision to start the programme, Boeing had still not

received a single order for the type.

The dam began to crumble in early 1955: in March of that year, the USAF ordered the Boeing KC-135 tanker/transport version; the US airlines then started to show active interest in jets, partly because the USAF was now committed to ironing out any early problems and (in Pan Am's case) because the Comet 4 was now on order and scheduled to be flying the North Atlantic from 1958. With the USAF order secured, Boeing diverted their sales efforts to the airlines. Douglas and Lockheed were already working in the area; the main sales targets were Pan American, TWA and the big domestic airlines such as United

and American.

In June 1955, Douglas "froze" the design of the DC-8, which was to be substantially bigger than the 367-80. Douglas had lost a lot of time by shelving the original DC-8 in 1953, but by offering a bigger aircraft they forced Boeing to scale up the 707 from 190,000 lb gross weight to 245,000 lb, thereby losing half their lead.

From the start of their programme, Douglas adopted a different approach from that of Boeing. The DC-8 airframe was designed so that it could be converted into an intercontinental aircraft with minimal changes as soon as sufficiently powerful engines became available, while

The Boeing 367-80 was designed from the outset as a dual-role aircraft, with the military need for flying tankers in mind. Here the 367-80 banks away behind an early US Air Force KC-135A Stratotanker

While Boeing produced a wide variety of different-sized 707s, all the Douglas DC-8s built before 1965 had similar dimensions to the prototype shown here

the Boeing 707-120, although smaller and more efficient than the first DC-8, was not an intercontinental aircraft and Boeing therefore had to develop a substantially modified version.

The Great Jet Race started in earnest in October 1955, when Pan Am ordered 20 of the initial 707 version, the 707-120, plus 25 Douglas DC-8s. The 707-120 was a 110-passenger, 2,700-mile range machine, and Pan Am wanted it by autumn 1958 to meet the challenge of BOAC's Comet 4s on one-stop transatlantic services. The 707-120 had 13,000 lb-thrust Pratt & Whitney JT3C-6s, civil versions of the J57. It was ten feet longer than the 367-80, with ten feet more wingspan,

and it introduced the Boeing-developed Kruger flap on the wing leading edge. This was a metal plate hinged at the front of the wing; swung out below the leading-edge for take-off, "it fooled the air into thinking there was a blunt leading-edge there," in the words of one engineer. It was fully retracted in cruising flight, unlike the slats fitted to the DC-8, allowing Boeing to build wings with sharper leading edges for good cruise efficiency. Every technical weapon was thrown into the life-and-death struggle between the Boeing and Douglas big jets. United Airlines bought 30 DC-8-10s, the domestic version of the Douglas jet, and said that one of their reasons was that they did not think

Boeing's fuselage was wide enough to seat six passengers. Boeing promptly redesigned the entire fuselage of the 707 to add four inches to the cabin width, clinching the sale of 30 707-120s to American Airlines.

By early 1956, Boeing were concerned that Douglas might be winning the race to build a jet which could fly the Atlantic non-stop. Pan Am's DC-8s, ordered in October 1955 along with the 707-120s, were to be intercontinental DC-8-30s, due in service from 1959. The DC-8-30 was to be fitted with Pratt & Whitney JT4As, giving up to 17,500 lb of thrust. This engine was a civil version of the military J75, big brother of the J57. It was a pure-jet engine, unlike its British rival, the

Rolls-Royce Conway, which had been developed specifically for the civil market and was the first "by-pass" engine, offering better efficiency. Like the JT4A, it offered up to 17,500 lb-thrust for the early intercontinental jets.

Boeing produced two "special-order" versions of the early 707, in contrast to the Douglas policy of standardisation. The 707-220 was a "hot-rod", JT4A-powered version of the 120 for Texas-based Braniff Airlines, and the 707-138 was a long-range aeroplane for Quantas, the Australian national carrier, with a body ten feet shorter than other 707s. The first true long-range version of the 707, however, was the 707-320, ordered by Pan Am in early

United Airlines were "launch customers" for the DC-8, putting Douglas back into the race with Boeing

113

above
Part of the reason for Boeing's success has been their willingness to develop special versions for particular requirements. The short-fuselage, long-range 707-138B was one such "one-off" for Qantas

right
Late customers for the Boeing 707-320C were Sudan Airways

1956 for North Atlantic operations. A 12 ft increase in wing-span and an eight feet fuselage stretch (compared with the 707-120) produced an aircraft fully the equal of the DC-8-30, with 150 seats and full, intercontinental range. Maximum take-off weight was almost exactly the same as that of the DC-8-30, at 312,000 lb. Orders for RR Conway-powered versions of both the 707 and DC-8 followed by the end of 1956:

Trans-Canada ordered the DC-8-40 in July 1956, and BOAC ordered the corresponding 707-420 the following November.

The first to fly was the 707-120, one of Pan Am's aircraft flying before the end of 1957. Pan Am started one-stop transatlantic operations via Gander in October 1958. The first DC-8, the prototype of United's DC-8-10, flew in May 1958, but the type did not enter

BOAC's first long-range jet was the specially developed 707-420, powered by early Rolls-Royce Conway bypass engines. The Super VC10 followed it into service in the mid-1960s, and both types were still in use when BOAC and BEA were merged into British Airways

The Italian flag carriers Alitalia were one of the few customers for the Douglas DC-8-40, powered by Rolls-Royce Conways rather than the normal Pratt & Whitney engines

service until September of the following year. The intercontinental DC-8-30 flew in November 1958, but was well and truly overhauled by the 707-320, which flew three months later and went into service in August 1959; the DC-8-30 and the Conway-powered DC-8-40 both carried their first fare-paying passengers in April 1960, one month after BOAC put the 707-420 into service.

Lockheed's jet studies came to nothing when the initial customers were scooped by Boeing and Douglas, but another US company – the Convair division of the General Dynamics Corporation – did decide to enter the four-jet market. Convair had built the highly successful 240/340/440 family of twin piston-engined airliners, as well as a series of sophisticated delta-wing supersonic military aircraft, but they

were relative newcomers to the world of large civil aircraft.

Convair started discussing their new airliner, provisionally called the Skylark, with TWA and Delta Air Lines in late 1955, and decided to go ahead with the aircraft on the basis of orders for 40 from these two airlines in September 1956. Re-designated the Convair 880, the new aircraft was very much the same size as Boeing's original 367-80 and was thus considerably smaller than the 707-120 or the DC-8-10. It weighed just under 190,000 lb at take-off (about three-quarters as much as the Boeing and Douglas jets) and was designed for one-stop trans-USA flights. It differed from its rivals in two significant ways: it had General Electric engines, a commercial version of the J79 designated CJ-805-3 and developing some 11,200 lb-thrust; and its fuselage was designed to seat five passengers abreast, rather than six.

The 880 made its maiden flight in January 1959 and went into service in May of the following year, by which time it was already clear that the 707 and DC-8 had pre-empted much of the market, and only some 50 Convairs were sold. Convair's response to the poor sales of the 880 was a typically bold gamble: in 1958, they announced a new version – the Convair Golden Arrow – which would not only fly further than the 880 but which would be substantially faster than any other jet airliner.

American ordered 25 of the type in July 1958.

Redesignated the Convair 990 Coronado, the new airliner flew in January 1960. Among its more unusual features were its aft-fan CJ-805-23 turbofan engines, basically consisting of a turbojet mounted in a duct with a free-spinning turbine wheel, with fan blades around its circumference, installed behind it. The wing had a relatively low aspect ratio (the ratio of span to chord) of 5.8:1, compared with 7.04:1 on the 707. The wing section was amazingly thin, to allow high

First of the Convair jets was the 880. Smaller and slimmer than the 707 and DC-8, the Convairs were powered by General Electric engines. Viasa of Venezuela were among the customers

After its early troubles, the Convair 990 established a fine record with operators such as Swissair, as a well-built and well-mannered aeroplane

Mach numbers without buffet: the depth of the wing was about eight per cent of the chord at the root, (14 per cent on the 707) tapering to five per cent at the tip. Four "Kuchemann carrot" fairings, named after the Farnborough scientist who invented them, were attached to the wing trailing edge to delay the formation of shock waves over the rear of the wing.

The appearance of the 990 worried Boeing severely. The actual saving of journey time possible with the 990 was not enormous, but in the hands of an astute airline sales department it could be a decisive weapon. In that case, all Boeing's US domestic customers would want Coronados for their transcontinental

sectors, where competition was extremely keen. Accordingly, Boeing produced a short-fuselage, stripped-down version of the 707-120, with an extended leading-edge at the root giving the wing a distinctive compound sweep and increasing the the maximum cruise speed towards Convair 990 levels. The original designation (707-020) gave way to the more simple Boeing 720 in airline service. The 720 was not quite as attractive as the 990, but the advantage of standardisation with the 707 and the JT3C appealed to many operators.

The 720 entered service with United in July 1960, while the 990 hit trouble. Excessive drag around the new, fatter engine

cowlings prevented the aircraft from attaining its design speed or range, and a number of customers cancelled their orders. Finally, the problems were solved and the 990 went into service in mid-1962, nearly a year behind schedule. Only 32 were sold, and General Dynamics wrote off a $200 million loss on the 880/990 programme – the biggest loss in US corporate history at the time. General Electric also bowed out of the commercial jet engine business, at least for the time being.

The 720 caused the abandonment of Boeing's early plans to build a smaller, four-jet airliner in the Convair 880 class. The original Douglas DC-9 project was in the same bracket, and was planned with four

Pratt & Whitney J52s. By the time the 990 had been driven off the market, the two remaining US manufacturers on the scene were well advanced with development of definitive intercontinental versions of the 707 and DC-8. Even before the introduction (in 1959–60) of the JT4A and Conway versions, it became clear that a further very useful performance benefit was obtainable from Pratt & Whitney's answer to the Conway, the JT3D. The new US engine was a bypass type of rather more advanced design than the Conway, and offered more power (18,000 lb-thrust in its early version) and better fuel consumption. The DC-8-50 and 707-320B both used the new engine, could take

With its thin-section wing, "Whitcomb bodies" on the trailing-edge and powerful aft-fan engines, the Convair 990 was a daring but unsuccessful attempt to produce an airliner considerably faster than its rivals

119

above
Visible in this view of a Swissair
Convair 990 are the concentric
inlets for its aft-fan engines, unique
in an airliner

right
The standard version of the DC-8
was the -50, with Pratt & Whitney
JT3D engines. Garuda of
Indonesia became customers,
partly due to their close connections
with Douglas' best European
clients, KLM

off at weights up to 330,000 lb and could link Europe non-stop with the US West Coast. The advantages of the new versions were obvious, and they quickly supplanted the Conway and JT4A versions on the production lines from 1962 onwards. Boeing sold JT3D-powered versions of the 720 and 707-120 (the 720B and -120B) and many older aircraft were fitted with the new engines.

By the early 1960s, the piston-engined airliner was virtually extinct on the world's major air routes:

across the Atlantic and Pacific oceans, from Europe via India to Australia and across the American continent. Spurred on by competition and prestige, the re-equipment was astonishingly fast, and this was not altogether a good thing. Accident rates with the early jets were high, as airlines learned the problems associated with their high landing speeds and advanced technology. Some airlines fuelled their jets with JP-4 gasoline, until a few accidents demonstrated the risk of fire inherent

above
Cascade-type thrust reversers were developed to cope with the high landing speeds of the early jets. "Daisy"-type nozzles helped to reduce the noise of pure-jet engines such as these

in wing engines and integral fuel
tanks, after which most operators
switched to JP-1 kerosene, which is
much less easy to ignite.

The fact that the jets flew more
miles than the slower, piston-engined
airliners in a year, and could carry
more passengers, led to a slump in
airline profits during the early 1960s,
because traffic grew only slowly to
fill the available capacity. The rapid
pace of re-equipment also affected
the manufacturers' profits. The
economics of building anything as
complex as a jet airliner depend on
the "learning curve" effect, whereby
each successive aircraft moving down
the production line is built in slightly
fewer man-hours than the one before.
But, because the airlines were
clamouring for jets and more jets as
soon as possible, Boeing and Douglas
forced up their production rates
during the first years of delivery
rather than risk losing customers to a
rival. The early 707s and DC8s
therefore cost considerably more to
make than the airlines were paying;

Boeing lost no less than $200 million
on its first full year of 707 deliveries,
and the entire 707/720 programme
did not move into the black until
1964. Douglas, which started behind
Boeing in the race, probably lost
even more, and it is questionable
whether the DC-8 ever made a great
deal of money.

Both the 707 and the DC-8 were
sold in convertible and freighter
versions in fairly large numbers. The
convertible passenger/freight
707-320C was certainly the most
popular version of the Boeing in the
later years of production, while
Douglas put a great deal of effort into
their pure freight DC-8F Jet Trader,
which for many years was the
mainstay of the world's specialised
cargo carriers. The main impact, of
the 707 and DC-8, however, has
been on the passenger market. Jet
travel proved so much more attractive than the piston-engined "stage-
coaches" that it turned into a fashion
– the "jet set" had arrived. More
importantly, jets actually turned

122

out to be cheaper to operate than the older types. Journeys were shorter, so seating densities could be increased; originally planned as a 140-seater, the 707 carried up to 189 passengers with some low-fare, charter operators. The scheduled airlines started to offer new, low, excursion fares to compete with the charter operators, and air travel started to expand dramatically.

One consequence of the failure of Lockheed to get into the jet market was that Boeing replaced them as one of the two main manufacturers. In the 1960s, there was a tendency for airlines to become established as Boeing or Douglas customers; Pan Am, TWA and Lufthansa, for instance, developed a strong preference for Boeing products, while Alitalia and KLM were loyal Douglas customers. Boeing and Douglas between them had sold several hundred four-jet airliners by 1964, and any attempt to compete with their established products at that stage was probably doomed to failure.

The DC-8F Jet Trader was the freighter version of the DC-8. One of these became the first British-registered aircraft of the type in 1975

That, however, was just what the British aircraft industry tried to do with the Vickers (later BAC) VC10.

Vickers had started to study the possibility of a non-stop transatlantic jet in 1951, when it seemed that the Comet would be available by the mid-1950s for sectors up to 2,700 miles. Rolls-Royce had run their first Conway bypass jet in 1950, and early Vickers designs followed the configuration of the Valiant bomber, with four engines buried in the wing roots. The Valiant had four Rolls-Royce Avons in a high-mounted wing, however, and (like Boeing) the Vickers team concluded that a low-set wing was more suitable for an airliner.

The basic Vickers V1000 design crystallised in early 1952 as a low-wing type with four buried Conways, which were then expected to yield about 13,000 lb-thrust. Like the Boeing 367-80, under design at about the same time, the Vickers V1000 was designed to meet a

military requirement as well as a commercial one: in this case, as a Royal Air Force military transport. The RAF specification demanded good runway performance, and the V1000 featured a large, compound-sweep wing. Construction of the first, military V1000 started in October 1952, but – like many British projects of the time – it suffered from official vacillation and, by mid-1955, the RAF had begun to feel that the Britannia might be more suitable. Meanwhile, Vickers tried to get BOAC to show firm interest in the civil version, designated VC7, but the State airline were of the opinion that the Britannia would be

A VC10 on approach shows off its full-span leading-edge slats and Fowler flaps

competitive on long-haul routes in the foreseeable future. The economics of the VC7 on intercontinental routes were not as attractive as those of the Britannia, and the whole programme was finally abandoned in November 1955. The first prototype, which had reached the final-assembly stage, was broken up for scrap. Eleven months later BOAC ordered Boeing 707-420s; Vickers felt that the VC7 could have done the same job and been in service earlier, and that the British project had fallen victim to a simple BOAC prejudice in favour of American airliners. From that time on, politics and emotions tended to dominate BOAC's relationship with the British aircraft industry.

The VC10, which brought this relationship to the point of a public dispute, emerged from design studies which had started before the VC7/V1000 met its untimely end. In 1955–56, Vickers were looking at an aircraft called the Vanjet, which would have used the Vanguard nose and fuselage with a new swept wing

and three, rear-mounted Avons. Initially, the Vanjet was conceived as an insurance, in case BEA and Trans-Canada decided to go pure-jet instead of buying Vanguards; with the turboprop type committed to development, however, Vickers revised the Vanjet to meet BOAC requirements.

In the late 1950s, BOAC was faced with the prospect of bringing jet services to the far-flung network of African and Far Eastern routes which they had inherited from the days of Imperial Airways. The American manufacturers, however, were far too preoccupied with squeezing the last drop of payload-range out of their aircraft to worry about performance out of hot, high-elevation airfields. In BOAC's view, a smaller aircraft than the 707 would offer better economics on a difficult network, because it could operate with something like its design payload most of the time.

During 1956, Vickers scaled up the Vanjet with three Conways and then redesigned it with four, in

VC10s in production at Weybridge. The British long-haul jet was too closely optimised to BOAC requirements, and only 55 were built

paired pods at the rear, with a T-tail mounted on top of the fin. The rear engine layout offered a quieter cabin but, more importantly, it allowed a completely clean wing, with no breaks for engines in the flaps or in the full-span flaps. As a result, the take-off and climb performance of the new aircraft, designated VC10, was expected to be outstanding.

In March 1957, a few months after ordering 707s, BOAC issued a specification for a complementary type to work their African and Eastern network, capable of carrying a 35,000 lb payload over 4,000 miles. In addition, the type had to be capable of operating with as little payload penalty as possible out of hot-and-high airports such as Kano, Nairobi and Johannesburg, as well as tackling some of BOAC's most difficult Eastern-route sectors with full payload. The specification was

·written around the VC10, and in May 1957, BOAC gave Vickers a letter of intent covering 35 of the type, with 20 options. At that time the VC10 was to be much the same size as a 707-120, with four 16,500 lb-thrust Conway R.Co.10s, a 2,700 sq ft wing and a maximum take-off weight of 247,000 lb. By the end of the year, however, it had been modified to give it a non-stop trans-atlantic range, with 18,500 lb-thrust R.Co.15s and 299,000 lb gross weight. It was now a direct rival for the American big jets, and BOAC planning appeared to envisage the 707 as an interim type. At the beginning of 1958, BOAC signed a contract for 35 aircraft, with 15 options.

With the adoption of the 21,000 lb Conway R.Co.42 in early 1960, it became possible to consider a stretched version of the VC10 for operations where the airfield condi-

tions were less demanding, so that runway performance could be traded for payload. The Super VC10 was 13 ft longer than the standard aircraft, and featured an extra fuel tank in its tailfin to restore range to the Standard levels.

The first Standard VC10 flew in June 1962, and the type went into service with BOAC in April 1964, following modifications to cure excessive cruise drag; but the seven-year gestation of the VC10 had allowed it to be overhauled by the American jets, which – in their JT3D-powered versions – offered significantly better economics than the British jet. With the world-wide expansion of 707 and DC-8 operations, many of the airfields where the VC10 would have been at an advantage were lengthened to accept the US jets, and the only customers (apart from BOAC) were British United Airways and East African

Airways; the VC10 might almost have been tailor-made for the latter's network.

In 1964, BOAC said that they wanted to cancel most of their VC10s and buy 707-320Bs instead. The airline's management wanted a written directive from the Minister of Aviation before they would buy the VC10 "against our commercial judgment." The fact that the VC10 had been designed to BOAC's own specification was not considered relevant. Eventually a compromise was reached, and BOAC were allowed to drop their VC10 options. By that time, however, nearly all hopes of selling the VC10 had vanished. Production continued slowly until 1970, when the last of the type was delivered to East African Airways. The VC10 proved enduringly popular with its passengers for its ride and cabin quietness and, throughout its life with BOAC, flew with a

The rear engines of the elegant British Aircraft Corporation VC10 permitted a remarkably clean wing, and contributed to the type's good runway performance

above
The prototype Il-62 heads a line-up of Russian types at the 1965 Paris air show, its Western debut

top
A British Airways Super VC10 runs up its engines at a London Heathrow test stand. Although commercially unsuccessful, the type was popular with passengers

left
The scene aboard the flight deck of a BOAC Super VC10 en route from Entebbe to Johannesburg, flying at 35,000 ft at Mach 0.84

greater proportion of its seats filled
than any other type.

One airline which backed the
turboprop for intercontinental services was Aeroflot; in April 1961 they
gained the distinction of operating
the world's largest airliner when
they introduced the mighty Tupolev
Tu-114 Rossiya (Russia). The
Tu-114 was derived from the Tu-95
Bear bomber by the same process
that produced the Tu-104 medium-
range jet from the Tu-16 Badger;
the wings and engine nacelles of the

bomber were retained, but dropped
from the mid to the low position
on a new, large-diameter fuselage.
The Tu-114 also had longer-chord
flaps than the bomber. Four vast
14,795 ehp Kuznetsov NK-12MV
turbo-props spinning eight-blade
contra-rotating propellers, drove the
415,000 lb 170/220-seat giant at well
over 500 mph, and gave it a range
of up to 5,500 miles. About 30
Tu-114s are believed to have been
built; the prototype, flown in
October 1957, caused something of

a sensation at the 1959 Paris Air Show, not least by virtue of its luxurious, "Trans-Siberian-Railway" compartmented interior.

Despite its monstrous appearance, the Tu-114 was a major achievement. The engines and propellers were particularly noteworthy, operating in a speed range which was thought in the West to be the province of pure-jet or turbofan engines. The designation Tu-114D was applied to an even simpler conversion of the Tu-95 bomber used by Aeroflot to operate a high-priority Moscow-Havana non-stop service.

It was still felt necessary for the Soviet Union to have an intercontinental jet airliner, however, and the Ilyushin Il-62 Classic was flown in 1963, only two years after the Tu-114 entered service with Aeroflot. The size and basic layout of the Il-62 corresponded closely to that of the Super VC10, with four, rear-mounted engines; but at nearly 365,000 lb, the Soviet aircraft was considerably heavier and it also lacked the leading-edge slats of the British aircraft. The prototype had Mikulin AM-3 turbojets, because the definitive Kuznetsov NK-8 turbofans were not ready in time for the first flight. The later, Il-62M was re-engined with 25,500 lb Soloviev D-30Ks, but – despite this extra power – the Il-62M had a generally inferior performance to comparable Western aircraft.

The Il-62 entered service in 1966, and was exported mainly to other Warsaw Pact countries. Some efforts were made to export the type outside the Communist bloc, but without success. In the mid-1970s, the Il-62 replaced the last of the Tu-114s, which operated on Aeroflot's high-density holiday routes until their retirement in 1976.

The battle of the big jets saw the US manufacturers regain the lead which they had briefly looked like losing in the early 1950s. A world-wide fleet of over 1,000 long-haul jets built up the international route system which is operated today, and paved the way for the smooth development of mass air transport.

Closely similar to the British VC10, Aeroflot's Ilyushin Il-62 was the Soviet Union's first long-haul jet airliner

Bus-stop

There was a keen debate within the aircraft and airline industries in the first half of the 1950s on the relative merits of the jet and the turboprop on short-haul air routes. The shorter the sector, the more time was spent taxiing, climbing or descending, and the less impact a high maximum speed had on the total journey time from airport to airport. A new generation of turboprop airliners would fly at nearly 400 mph, not much slower than the jets, would have better runway performance than any jet aircraft then in service and would cost far less to operate.

British European Airways, which had been convinced of the merits of the turboprop in 1950, approached Vickers for their thoughts on a high-capacity Viscount successor in April 1953. At that time, Vickers were studying the Viscount 850, a stretched version with four Rolls-Royce RB.109s (later named the Tyne), but the aircraft quickly grew beyond the maximum size for a stretched Viscount. After two years of discussion, Vickers came up with the Type 870, sharing the Viscount's basic layout, but substantially bigger. The 870 had a double-bubble fuselage section rather than the simple circle of the Viscount, because BEA wanted more freight capacity in the lower hold, and it would carry 88 passengers in a BEA mixed layout.

Meanwhile, Trans-Canada Airlines had a requirement for a medium-range aircraft, and – like BEA – were not quite certain whether to go for jets or turboprops.

left
Late-1950s modernism in the cabin of the Vanguard

134

The TCA influence, together with the anticipated power growth available from the Tyne, led to a steady enlargement of what was now the Vickers Type 900. By July 1956, when BEA ordered 20 of the type for delivery in 1960, the version on offer to TCA weighed 141,000 lb for take-off and could seat 139 passengers in a high-density layout. The BEA version was designated the

951, and the new aircraft was named the Vanguard.

The jet Caravelle had flown one year before the Vanguard was ordered and although BEA still felt that the jet would not be needed except on their longer routes, they drafted a jet specification in 1957 which eventually produced the Trident. By 1958, with the Vanguard nearing completion, BEA decided

The second generation Vickers Vanguard propeller-turbine aircraft was produced at Weybridge in 1958–64. BEA took delivery of six Type 951 s (one of which is illustrated here)

The Lockheed Electra was the fastest turboprop airliner, but suffered a number of serious accidents. By the time the problems were solved, the jets were on the way

that most of their Vanguards should be 953s, optimised for short sectors. The Vanguard flew in 1959, but by this time it was clear that BEA and Vickers had made a mistake in going ahead with a second-generation turboprop. Problems with the Tyne (and few of the big turboprops were developed smoothly) delayed services until March 1961, and TCA and BEA remained the only customers. Many Vanguards were later converted into freighters.

Lockheed had a very similar experience. Discussions about a fast turboprop replacement for the DC-6s and Constellations on US domestic routes started in late 1954,

and Lockheed succeeded in persuading American Airlines and Eastern Airlines that the L-188 Electra offered more potential than the proposed four-jet DC-9 or a comparable Boeing specification. Ordered in mid-1955, the first Electra flew in late 1957 and went into service at the beginning of 1959. It looked similar to the Vanguard, but it was considerably smaller, weighing 116,000 lb against the 141,000 lbs of the Vanguard and it came with 3,750 ehp Allison 501D-13s (civil versions of the T56 fitted to Lockheed's C-130 Hercules freighter) compared to the Vanguard's 5,500 ehp Tyne R.Ty.11s. An interesting feature of the US design was its relatively short wing-span, chosen so that the Fowler flaps could be washed over their whole span by the propeller slipstream. This gave the Electra an outstanding runway performance: it could take off in 5,000 ft, compared with 6,200 ft for the Vanguard.

Lockheed took orders for 176 Electras in the early days of the programme, but two Electras broke up in flight and the aircraft was grounded while Lockheed tried to work out what had happened. The problem was eventually traced to violent oscillation of the propellers, and the Electra was modified to counter the problem. By the time the modified L-188A entered service in mid-1961, however, the type's reputation had suffered and many US airlines were committed to jets. No more L-188s were ordered, although Eastern operated the type successfully for many years. Lockheed, meanwhile, used the Electra

airframe, strengthened and suitably modified, as the basis for their very successful Orion anti-submarine patrol aircraft.

The Soviet Union's aircraft industry produced two medium-size turboprop airliners for Aeroflot. Whereas the service lives of the Vanguard and Electra were restricted by competition from the jets, this problem did not arise in a controlled economy; in this sense, the Soviet turboprops were more successful than their Western counterparts.

The first of the Soviet aircraft to enter service was the Ilyushin Il-18 Moskva, a very similar aircraft to the Vanguard in weight and speed. Powerplants were four Ivchenko AI-20s of 4,000 ehp. Flown in 1957, the Il-18 entered service with Aeroflot in April 1959; it was still extensively used up to the end of the 1970s, because many Russian airfields were still too short to accept

The Ilyushin Il-18, first flown in 1957, was one of the Soviet Union's most successful aircraft, selling to many African, Cuban and other airlines, albeit all within the Soviet sphere of influence

opposite
An early BEA Trident touches down:
the type was the first to be designed
for wholly automatic landing

Aeroflot's jets, with their generally high landing speeds. Like the Electra, it was later modified as an anti-submarine patrol aircraft. Il-18s were exported extensively to Cuba, Africa and to countries within the European communist bloc.

The other medium turboprop used by Aeroflot was the Antonov An-10 Ukraina of similar weight, size and capacity to the Il-18 and using the same engines, but designed to operate from short, undeveloped strips. It was basically an airliner version of the standard An-12 military freighter, sharing its high-set wing and fuselage-mounted main undercarriage. Double-slotted flaps were fitted to the wing, which featured the anhedral (drooped) outer sections which had become an Antonov trademark. The An-10 entered service in July 1959 and served in limited numbers until 1972, when faults in the wing structure caused a number of accidents and the type was retired. Both Soviet turboprops carried 100/120 passengers, but the Il-18 had a slightly longer range than the An-10. Interestingly, in 1978 Lockheed offered a passenger version of their Hercules freighter, by the same process that had produced the An-10 from the An-12 some 20 years earlier.

In the competitive West, however, airline executives were deciding that it was time to apply the technology of the early long-haul jets to their shorter routes. A design feature which was to distinguish two of the Western contenders in the market made its first appearance in 1949, when the American Martin company unveiled their experimental XB-51 light bomber. Among its many unusual features was the engine installation, with two jet engines on pylons below the forward fuselage and a third buried in the extreme tail and fed by an intake at the base of the fin. The tailplane was fitted at the top of the fin, Martin having been one of the pioneers of this "T-tail" arrangement.

It appears that Vickers were the first manufacturers to decide that the right number of engines for short-to-medium-range was more than two but less than four. Some airlines were very doubtful about the wisdom of relying on two engines for what were, by piston-engined standards, fairly large aircraft, but the twin-engined layout offered the best economics. A return to the three-engined layout, virtually extinct since the early 1930s (with exceptions such as some Italian aircraft and the Junkers Ju52/3m) seemed to be an attractive compromise. The Vickers Vanjet project of 1955–56 was the first design to combine the buried tail engine of the XB-51 with the side-mounted engines of the Caravelle.

Vickers moved from the Vanjet to a larger aircraft aimed at a BOAC requirement, as related in the previous chapter, but British European Airways were sufficiently interested to put out a specification for an 80-seat "trijet" in 1957. The aircraft was to be in service by 1964, and had to be faster than the Caravelle. Development was slightly delayed by the insistence of the British Government that the aircraft must be built by a consortium of companies: the Government had realised that the industry could not support the large number of individual firms then in existence, and was using its control of the state airlines to bring the manufacturing industry into line.

By the end of 1957, there were three contenders for the BEA requirement: the Bristol 200, with three Olympus turbojets at the rear, Vanjet-style, but also making use of the T-tail arrangement; the Avro 740, with three Olympus in rear-fuselage pods, the centre engine mounted on top of the fuselage between two sweptback "butterfly" tail surfaces; and the de Havilland D.H.121, similar in layout to the Bristol 200, but powered by Rolls-Royce RB.140 bypass engines. The de Havilland contender was selected in February 1958, by which time it had grown into a 110-seater aircraft weighing 130,000 lb, with a range of 1,500 miles. By early 1959, the type had grown again to nearly 150,000 lb, with three 14,000 lb-thrust RB.141s, now named the Medway. The D.H.121 was christened the Trident.

In March 1959, BEA decided that the Trident as it was then emerging was much too big for their needs, and that they would not sign a production contract unless the aircraft was scaled down. With hindsight, de Havilland might have done better to tell BEA to go and make the aeroplane they wanted elsewhere, and to carry on with the D.H.121 as it was; but at the time, the Boeing 727 was very far from a firm programme, and some people within de Havilland were themselves worried about the way the D.H.121 was growing inexorably into the Convair 880-size bracket. Accordingly, the aircraft was pushed down to the original 80 seats, and designed for minimum costs-per-aircraft-mile on BEA's European network. This meant that the Trident was optimised for sectors of less than 1,000 miles, using 10,000 ft sea-level runways in temperate climates. The powerplant of the new, smaller version, ordered by BEA in August 1959, was a 9,800 lb-thrust, scaled-down Medway, the RB.163 Spey. One very advanced feature specified for the Trident was fully automatic landing for year-round operations in foggy, cloudy Northern Europe. BEA wanted to be able to land their Tridents in zero visibility, which meant that the automatic systems had to be as reliable as the structure: there had to be only a 10^{-7} probability of failure. This required the installation of three complete autopilots, so that if one failed the other two could "vote" it out of operation. It took 13 years to develop the system fully, by which time the emergence of digital electronics had made the Trident hardware obsolete.

About the time that BEA and de Havilland were scaling down the Trident, Boeing were beginning to think about a smaller companion for the 707 family. The basic frame of reference had been set up in 1958, when the company formed a 727 planning office under Jack Steiner. The new aircraft had to be smaller than either the 707 or its smaller derivative, the 720; it had to operate from smaller airfields, including the many 7,500 ft fields in the USA; and – because it would operate on

shorter stage lengths – it would have to be designed to give its best performance at lower cruising altitudes. Its rivals would be the Caravelle, the Electra and the Douglas DC-9 project, which was still a baby DC-8 with four engines at that time.

The main market was among the US domestic airlines, and Boeing again started on the paper-aeroplane game, trying to reach a design which would be acceptable to all their major customers; otherwise, any airline which felt that its own requirements had been ignored was likely to place an order for rival aircraft in a fit of pique. Similarly, a modification made at the request of one airline may be unacceptable to another.

Boeing's problem by early 1959 was that United, the biggest of the US trunk airlines, was insisting that only a four-engined aircraft could offer satisfactory performance out of Denver airport, 5,300 ft above sea level and a vital link in the airline's network. But Boeing were not interested in a four-engined aircraft, because that would compete too closely with the 720. By mid-1959, United seemed likely to buy the four-engined DC-9, and Boeing were beginning to worry about a possible slump in orders once the initial boom in 707 deliveries wore off in 1963–64. The company oscillated between two and four engines, as well as studying three-engined aircraft, which appealed to the market but appeared awkward from the design viewpoint. By September 1959, however, the company had decided that the right number of engines probably was three, and – after looking at a design with two engines under the wing and a third in the tail (the layout later adopted for the wide-body trijets) – they settled on a layout with all three engines at the rear. By September 1959, the 727 was much the same size as the aircraft which eventually emerged, but featured a mid-height tailplane and a landing gear retracting rearwards into Tupolev-style pods on the trailing edge of the wing.

At the turn of 1960, Boeing were

still far from happy about investing many millions of dollars in what would inevitably be a risky programme, especially after the heavy losses incurred in the early years of 707 production. Boeing discussed collaboration with Sud-Aviation on the Caravelle and with de Havilland on the Trident; after United's order for Caravelles, the US manufacturers were extremely worried about the threat posed by the European companies' lower labour rates. In February 1960, the Boeing board decided that they would go ahead with the 727 if they could get orders from United and Eastern, who wanted to use their 727s from the 5,000 ft runway at New York's La Guardia airport.

Through most of 1960, it seemed extremely likely that the 727 would have Rolls-Royce Medways built under licence by Allison, until Pratt & Whitney offered a new turbofan based on their military J52 turbojet.

The JT8D offered more power than the 727 really needed, but Boeing decided to use it "derated", allowing a margin for future growth. Eastern and United switched to the Pratt & Whitney engine in August, by which time Boeing were virtually committed to going ahead if a total of 100 orders was obtained by the end of that November.

Meanwhile, Boeing had decided that the mid-set tailplane was not offering satisfactory handling characteristics, and changed to a T-tail; they were almost certainly influenced by the Trident, which de Havilland had allowed them to inspect in detail while the two companies were discussing possible collaboration. Boeing also switched to an inward-retracting undercarriage, leaving the wing clean.

The 727 as it was by late 1960 was very similar in weight, thrust, capacity and range to the original, Medway-powered Trident, and was

141

Kuwait Airways were one of a few export customers for the Trident

thus substantially larger than the aircraft then under development for BEA. The main difference between the two aircraft, apart from size, was that the 727 was designed with a highly sophisticated range of high-lift devices on the wing, increasing the cost but resulting in a far more flexible aircraft. The Trident was fitted in its early versions with a double-slotted trailing-edge flap and a simple drooping leading edge (later Tridents had full-span slats); the 727 featured massive, triple-slotted flaps on the trailing edge, with Kruger flaps on the inboard wing and slats outboard, and this combined efficient cruising at medium altitudes (which dictated a small wing) with approach speeds no higher than the DC-7s it was expected to replace. Boeing even tested a flap-blowing system, using air drawn from the engines to increase lift by diverting high-pressure air over the flaps. The system was tried out on the long-suffering 367-80, but was felt to be too complex and expensive. The arrangement of flaps eventually chosen for the 727 was also flown on the 367-80, together with a representative side nacelle; Boeing wanted to make certain that the complex flaps would not cause turbulent flow and affect the working of the rear engine.

United and Eastern signed orders for 80 727s on the last day of November 1960, just before the deadline set by the Boeing board, and the company decided to relax their commitment to a 100-order launch and to go ahead with the programme anyway. Other orders followed in rapid succession, in-

cluding one from Lufthansa, the first European national carrier to order the type.

Despite the fact that the Trident had been ordered 15 months earlier than the 727, the first aircraft did not fly until December 1961; flight-testing of the Boeing jet proceeded faster than that of the Trident, and both types entered airline service early in 1964. By that time, the Boeing 727 was clearly showing its superiority over its British rival, despite a rash of early crashes caused because pilots were unfamiliar with the behaviour of the high-lift wing; excessive sink rate could be catastrophic if not corrected quickly. Like the big jets, the 727 was less forgiving than its piston-engined predecessors, and had to be flown strictly "by the book", rather than by the "seat of the pants".

Aware that the decision to scale down the Trident had been a mistake, de Havilland offered an enlarged Trident, the 1A, to American Airlines. American had lagged behind its US rivals in buying the 727 but, despite the British offer, they joined the queue of Boeing customers. BEA remained the only major Trident customer, and development continued with the medium-range Trident 2E. BEA and Lufthansa were the only European carriers to order trijets in the early days; Air France had their Caravelles, and the other airlines, such as KLM and Alitalia, were looking for smaller aircraft to replace their DC-6s and Convair twins.

The first of several small twinjet types to fly did so in the Soviet Union in December 1959 and, in 1962, it became the first small turbo-

A 727-100 of US regional carrier Piedmont Airlines. The importance of this group of carriers increased markedly throughout the 1960s and 1970s

The Tupolev Tu-124, a scaled-down
version of the Tu-104, was the first
short-range jet with by-pass engines

fan airliner to enter service. The Tupolev Tu-124 Cookpot was basically a scaled-down Tu-104 Camel, with the same, sharply-swept wings, wing-root engines and wing-mounted undercarriage. It was, however, a great deal smaller, with up to 65 seats in a high-density layout. It weighed just over 65,000 lb and was powered by two 11,000 lb-thrust Soloviev D-20 turbofans. Aeroflot did use the Tu-124, but not in very large numbers – it was designed as much as a fast military/ VIP transport as for commercial use, and was overshadowed by a rear-engined airliner developed from it. Initially designated Tu-124B, the new type became the Tu-134 before its first flight, as the commonality between it and its forbear decreased. Powered by two uprated D-30Ks, giving up to 15,000 lb-thrust in later versions, the Tu-134 went into service in 1967, to be followed by the stretched Tu-134A. The small Tupolev twinjet, carrying up to 80 passengers, became the standard short-haul

vehicle of Aeroflot and of the airlines of the Warsaw Pact countries. The wing configuration, with 36° of sweep and crude high-lift devices, was still the same as that of the Tu-104 (and its military ancestor the Tu-16). A high ratio of power to weight helped the aircraft achieve a reasonable take-off run, but its landing speed was very high compared with Western contemporaries and mishaps were quite common. An unusual feature of the Tu-134 was a large, door-type airbrake under the centre section, but this was later removed from many aircraft because it could not be retracted quickly enough if the pilot decided to overshoot a landing. The Tu-134A remained in production until the mid-1970s.

The first of the small, Western twinjets was developed from design studies and market research carried out by a small British company, Hunting Percival, in the mid-1950s. In 1955, the company produced plans for a small airliner, the H.75,

A unique feature of the Tupolev Tu-134 was its ventral speedbrake

powered by two, 4,000 lb-thrust Bristol Orpheus engines of the type developed for the Gnat light fighter. By 1958, when the company were taken over by the British Aircraft Corporation (which also comprised Vickers and English Electric) the project had become the H.107 with two Bristol BE.75 turbofans and about 60 seats. The design then became the responsibility of BAC at Weybridge, where it was seen as a very promising Viscount replacement. However, it was not certain that the BE.75 engine would materialise, so the design was scaled up once again to accept the Rolls-Royce Spey, which by that time was firmly under development for the Trident. Using the Hunting numbering system, the new type became the BAC 111, pronounced and written as One-Eleven. In May 1961, BAC decided to go ahead with the One-Eleven following an order for ten from British United Airways. BUA were a new airline, formed the previous year from the merger of several small independent British carriers.

above
Soviet counter to the Western twinjets was the rear-engined Tu-134, but the type did not sell outside the Soviet bloc

left
Britain's most successful jet was the BAC One-Eleven. More than 220 were sold

opposite, top
Even in the 1960s, test-flying was not without incident. This One-Eleven prototype force-landed on Salisbury Plain

opposite, bottom
The One-Eleven production line in late 1968. The range was extended by the addition of the stretched 500 and the short-field 475 series

The initial BUA version, the One-Eleven 200, was a 70-seater which could carry up to 89 passengers in a high-density arrangement and it was designed for 500-mile sectors. The One-Eleven 300 was heavier, with greater fuel capacity, and could carry a full load for more than 1,000 miles. In fact, the 300 was never built, as production concentrated on the 400, with similar performance but slight modifications to meet US airworthiness requirements. In 1962, American Airlines and Mohawk Airlines (the latter was later absorbed into Allegheny) placed substantial orders for the One-Eleven 400 in the absence of any comparable US type. The One-Eleven had built up a considerable lead over the competition by the time the prototype flew in May 1963, although some of

147

the lead was lost when the first aircraft crashed a few months later during flight tests. The aircraft fell victim to "deep-stall", a phenomenon unique to T-tailed aircraft. Under certain conditions the wing would stall, and the turbulent airflow from the stalled wing would blanket the high-set tailplane. The rear engines contributed to this blanketing effect, with the result that the elevators were ineffective and the normal recovery action from a stall (pushing the nose down) was impossible. If the stall was taken beyond a certain point, the One-Eleven – and most other T-tailed, rear-engined jets – would simply drop out of the sky. After the One-Eleven accident, most T-tailed jets were fitted with a stall-warning system which caused the control wheel to shake violently if the aircraft approached a stall. If the pilot still failed to push the wheel forward, the warning system would do it for him.

When the One-Eleven entered service in late 1964, its first US competitor was already flying. Douglas had been left behind in the race to replace most of the medium-range, piston-engined types in the US airline fleet by the speed of Boeing's 727 launch, and they were experiencing the slow-down in the big-jet market that Boeing had predicted in 1959. Douglas had gone further in discussions with Sud-Aviation than had Boeing and, even in 1961, there was still a chance that Douglas would build an Americanised Caravelle with aft-fan General Electric CJ805-23s as a smaller competitor for the 727. However, like Boeing, Douglas became convinced that they could make a better aircraft than the eight-year-old Caravelle, and the talks with Sud-Aviation came to nothing. In 1962, Douglas showed the airlines a project called the D-2086. It was basically similar to the One-Eleven but slightly larger, being designed around the 12,000 lb-thrust JT8D rather than the 10,500 lb-thrust Spey. The fuselage section was double-bubble, rather than circular like that of the One-Eleven, although both aircraft were designed to seat five passengers abreast. Both aircraft were rear-engined, T-tail types with moderately swept wings (25° on the Douglas, and 20° on the slightly slower One-Eleven); neither had any leading-edge devices in their initial versions, the One-Eleven having single-section Fowler flaps and the D-2086 double-slotted flaps.

The D-2086 became the DC-9-10, which made its first flight in 1964, but McDonnell Douglas were already offering considerably stretched versions of the basic design by that time. They were able to do this because the JT8D was basically a 14,000 lb-thrust engine running below its design rating, so that the DC-9 had a great deal of power in reserve. The most important of the stretched versions was the DC-9-30, with accomodation for up to 125 passengers in a high-density layout. The fuselage was 15 ft longer than that of the DC-9-10, and the wing featured extended tips and full-span slats on the leading-edge. The DC-9-30 had a range of about 1,500 miles with a full passenger load, and later versions had more fuel, higher take-off weights and an even longer range. Eastern Airlines placed a major order for DC-9-30s in February 1965, and Delta Air Lines also became a major operator of the type, but it was in Europe that the DC-9-30 made its greatest impact, with many of the area's flag carriers buying the type. Alitalia, KLM and Swissair became DC-9-30 operators, while Scandinavian Airlines System bought both the "hot-rod" DC-9-20 – with the -30 wing and engines and the -10 fuselage – and the DC-9-40, which was slightly longer even than the -30. The DC-9-20 remained unique to SAS, while the DC-9-40 was later bought by Toa Domestic Airlines in Japan.

With such a variety of improved models on the market, DC-9 sales rocketed. By the end of 1966 Douglas had orders for 400. The speed of the Douglas counter-attack took BAC

by surprise, and the Spey was not powerful enough to allow a stretched One-Eleven of comparable performance. It was already too late to re-engine the One-Eleven with the JT8D, which might have produced a European rival to the DC-9-30; in any case it was unlikely that airlines like KLM, with a tradition of buying Douglas products for more than 30 years, would be interested in such an aircraft. The One-Eleven remained cheaper and more efficient than the smaller DC-9s, however, and carved itself a useful niche in the lower end of the market. In 1967, BAC flew the stretched One-Eleven 500, a 119-seater designed for BEA, and sales of the type continued slowly right through the mid-1970s. The One-Eleven thus became the second best-selling European jet behind the Caravelle, with just over 220 sales.

By early 1964, BAC was not the only company worried by the apparently irresistible rise of the DC-9. Boeing could see that the greater capacity of the DC-9-30 could make serious inroads into the 727 market; if 727 operators bought the twinjets, they might be tempted to add more DC-9s to their fleets instead of the bigger 727s, which tended to be more costly over short sectors. By 1964, Boeing had some spare design manpower, as their supersonic transport was some way in the future and the 727 design was complete, and they started looking at twinjets. The Boeing solution, worked out in the summer of 1964, just as the DC-9 started its flight tests, was different from the other two twinjets. The 737 was to have the same body cross-section as the 707 and 727, seating six passengers abreast, and engines

above
The DC-9-40, slightly longer than the DC-9-50, was ordered only by Scandinavian Airlines System and Toa Domestic Airways

opposite, top
Many of the original DC-9-10s were replaced by later versions with their purchasers, and the -10s sold to charter airlines such as Spantax in the 1970s

opposite, bottom
The most popular version of the DC-9 was the -30, first ordered by Eastern Airlines. It is also used by many European carriers, including Swissair, Alitalia and KLM

151

slung directly beneath the wing rather than on pylons or at the rear. The engines would be JT8Ds, confirming the Pratt & Whitney engine as the most successful powerplant of the jet age.

The first customer for the 737 was Lufthansa, who badly needed a small aircraft to feed traffic from the major German industrial cities to Frankfurt, where their international flights originated. By the end of 1964, Boeing were in a quandary, because Lufthansa were threatening to buy DC-9s if Boeing did not make the 737, but Boeing wanted orders from some of the big US airlines before committing themselves to the twinjet. In February 1965, Boeing finally agreed to build the 737 on the basis of an order from Lufthansa alone; in the same month, Eastern Airlines, one of the US prospects for the 737, bought DC-9-30s.

Eventually, in April, United Airlines ordered 30 stretched 737-200s, comparable to the DC-9-30 and seating up to 130 passengers (the US airlines operated the 737-200 and DC-9-30 with about 100 mixed-class seats). Lufthansa turned out to be the only major customer for the basic 737-100, which was one of Boeing's less successful designs and which suffered from severe drag problems. United were the only major US carrier to order large numbers of 737s, because the type ran foul of a ruling by the US pilots' union that aircraft in that class had to be flown by three-pilot crews; the DC-9 was introduced before the pilots made this move, and could be flown in the USA with a two-man crew (as 737s were flown by non-US operators). This artificially improved the economics of the DC-9 compared with the Boeing twin.

The 737 only took off after a programme of minor improvements produced the Advanced 737-200 in the early 1970s. Unlike the DC-9, it was available in freighter-convertible form, and this – together with its rough-field capability – made it particularly attractive in the "third world" or in any tough operating environment.

In 1965–66, however, the DC-9 was the undisputed market leader

and, paradoxically, was making Douglas bankrupt. In order to secure customers for the type and to wipe out the One-Eleven's lead, Douglas salesmen offered a wide range of options, and promised early delivery dates to all their customers. The company was therefore having to deliver a great many aircraft from the top of the "learning curve"; that is to say, the workers were unused to the processes involved and each aircraft was taking far more manhours than Douglas planned to achieve later in the programme. The problem was compounded by the multiplicity of different versions, different internal arrangements, and different paint schemes. Because the aircraft were taking longer to build, they were also costing more, and the company were offering low "introductory" prices to most of their customers.

All this would have been bad enough without the fact that the Vietnam War had started, and was creating a boom in the US aerospace business. Component manufacturers were busy, and bits of the DC-9 contracted out to other manufacturers were arriving behind schedule. What was worse, the pool of semi-skilled labour – experienced in the manufacture and assembly of aircraft, and on which all California-based aircraft companies rely – had dried up. The cost to Douglas of each DC-9 was rocketing, and it became clear that deliveries were going to slip behind schedule; the airline customers were therefore threatening lawsuits for breach of contract to recover their lost revenue. At the end of 1966, Douglas ran out of money, and were taken over by the McDonnell Corporation. DC-9 deliveries were brought on schedule by sheer brute force, but the McDonnell Douglas Aircraft Company became much more cautious in their dealings. Douglas were the first of three US airliner manufacturers to go to the brink of disaster in the space of five years. After the take-over, the DC-9 went from strength to strength and, at the time of writing, was the best-selling twinjet.

Rather smaller than its US and British rivals, the Fokker F.28 was

designed as a jet successor to the
Friendship in 1962–63 and flown in
1966. The original Mk 1000 was a
65-seater; the later, stretched versions could carry up to 85 passengers.
The powerplant was the Rolls-Royce
Spey Junior, a 9,000 lb-thrust engine
developed from the larger Spey with
some components of the military
RB.168. Fokker hoped to continue
their co-operation with Fairchild-
Hiller in the USA; it was planned
that Fairchild should build the
F-228, a smaller version of the F.28
powered by advanced Rolls-Royce
Trent turbofans, but this project
was dropped in its early stages.
The F.28 was unique among these
jets in using a tail-mounted split

airbrake rather than thrust reversers;
some versions were also fitted with
leading-edge slats. Sales of the F.28
did not go quite as well as Fokker
had hoped, but the type sold fairly
well to smaller carriers.

The Soviet Union was late on the
scene with a medium-range jet transport in the class of the 727, and the
aircraft which finally filled this role
for Aeroflot, the Tupolev Tu-154,
was rather larger than the US trijet.
First flown in 1967, the Tu-154
closely resembled the 727 and Trident in basic layout, with three rear
engines and a T-tail, but its landing
gear consisted of six-wheel bogies
retracting rearwards into the now
traditional Tupolev pods. Power-

Linjeflyg were among the most important customers for the Fokker F.28, which they used on domestic services in Sweden. Because of its low noise, the F.28 was the only jet permitted to use Stockholm Bromma airport

plants were three Kuznetsov NK-8s of about 21,000 lb-thrust, as fitted to early Il-62s. It was the first Soviet airliner to feature high-lift devices on the Western pattern, with triple-slotted trailing-edge flaps and full-span slats on the leading edge. However, it soon became clear that the system was not as thoroughly developed as that on the 727, and early Tu-154s suffered from very serious control and stability problems. Plans to develop a stretched version seating 250 passengers – the Tu-154M – were abandoned while the design bureau attempted to cure the problems of the standard aircraft. The original Tu-154 had to carry as much as six tons of ballast when operating at maximum weight, in order to balance the aircraft with a full load of fuel in the wings. The later Tu-154A included a number of modifications, allowing the ballast to be carried as fuel (this was cited as an advantage, in that the fuel could be picked up where it was cheap, and used to replenish the tanks in a high-cost area). Egyptair, the only customer for the early Tu-154 outside the Warsaw Pact, returned their aircraft to the Soviet Union after one of them crashed during a training flight. The later Tu-154B, introduced in 1976, had modified ailerons and spoilers, and a maximum take-off weight of 220,000 lb. The type has a typical mixed-class capacity of 165 passengers, and is used extensively by Aeroflot on its medium-haul international routes, despite its shortcomings. In fact, the Tu-154B now appears to be satisfactory and in 1977 production was actually increased.

left
Tupolev Tu-154s in final assembly. The type is one of the most numerous Soviet airliners

below
An Aeroflot Tu-154A at Moscow, with a Tu-154B behind it. The safety record of the Tupolev trijet has led to a series of improved versions of the type

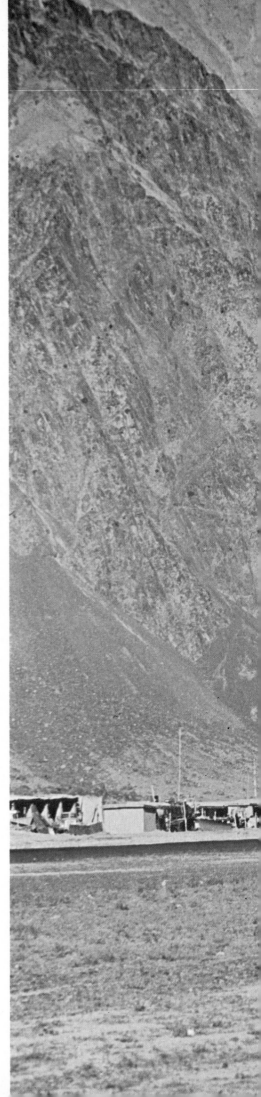

above
The Dassault Mercure resembled a longer-bodied 737. It appeared much later then the US twins and only ten were sold

right
Fokker's little F.28 proved highly suited to the most inhospitable terrain, as this Fokker-owned aircraft demonstrates at a mountain airfield

The French aircraft industry made two unsuccessful attempts to make up for the opportunity lost by their failure to develop the Caravelle. In the mid-1960s, the Caravelle was put into production with JT8Ds and a stretched fuselage, but only a few of these Caravelle 10s and 12s were sold. It was a 110-seater in the DC-9-30 class, but the smaller wings of the US twinjets made them more efficient than the Caravelle.

Even less successful was the Dassault Mercure. The Dassault company, famous for their Mirage fighters, started looking at the market for airliners in the mid-1960s and

An abortive challenge to the US twinjets was the Caravelle Super, flown experimentally with aft-fan engines similar to those of the Convair 990

concluded that there was a gap in that market for an aircraft in the same general category as the US twinjets, but with a greater capacity and shorter range. The company received French Government backing for the project, and got an order from Air Inter, the government-owned domestic airline. The Mercure, which made its first flight in 1972 and went into service two years later, was not unlike the 737 in appearance, except that its fuselage was longer and its JT8D engines were carried on pylons instead of being attached directly to the wing. It could carry up to 135 passengers over an 800-mile stage, but suffered from inflexibility; it was very difficult to trade payload for range without spoiling the economics of the aircraft. An interesting feature of the Mercure was its cockpit head-up display, a military development used on an airliner for the first time.

Dassault had reckoned without the "stretchability" of the DC-9. In 1973, Swissair placed the first order for the DC-9-50, yet another version of the McDonnell Douglas twinjet, aimed at the very large-capacity, short-range market which Dassault had identified. Some 80 DC-9-50s were sold; the type could carry up to 139 passengers at high density and was at its best over stage lengths of less than 800 miles. Sales were limited, however, due to the fact that the -50 was noisier than earlier DC-9s, and airlines changing from one type to the other became unpopular with local communities. But

the appearance of the DC-9-50
sealed the fate of the Mercure, and
the Dassault production line closed
in 1975 following the delivery of the
last of Air Inter's ten aircraft.

In 1975, therefore, the twinjet
market was dominated by the DC-9
(800 aircraft sold) and the 737 (more
than 300 sold); the Europeans had a
tenuous toehold with the One-Eleven
500 and 475 (the latter combining
the short, 400 fuselage and the
slightly longer wing of the 500) and
with the F.28 series, but the American superiority was almost complete.
In only one area would the Europeans issue any sort of a challenge to
the US industry – supersonic flight.

Swissair were the launch airline for
the stretched DC-9-50

The supersonic adventure

One of the oldest axioms in the aviation industry is that by the time an aircraft enters service, its replacement should be on the drawing board. The vast costs of developing new aircraft have made this practically impossible since the Second World War, but in any company there is always somebody thinking "what comes next?" as the first delivery ceremony takes place.

In the early 1950s, it was accepted in many quarters that the next stage after jets would be the supersonic airliner. The possibility that the industry might move to far greater capacity and lower fares seemed much more remote than the prospect of an airliner cruising at more than the speed of sound. The jets, people reasoned, had followed the performance trends set by military jet bombers; by the early 1950s, the armed forces on both sides of the Atlantic were studying supersonic bombers – Convair received a contract for their XB-58 in 1953 – and the supersonic transport (SST) could not be far behind.

Two Boeing engineers looked at the possibility of an SST in 1952 and concluded that the company "should take another look at it in 30 years' time." (One of the two, R. D. FitzSimmons, is, at the time of writing, heading the McDonnell Douglas SST study team.) Within two years of this statement, however, aerodynamicists at the Royal Aircraft Establishment, Farnborough, started a series of studies which led directly to the world's first and so far only technically successful supersonic airliner.

This was only seven years after the first controlled level flight through the sound barrier by a manned aircraft. The Bell XS-1, which achieved this in October 1947, was a tiny, rocket-powered aircraft with a bullet-like fuselage and razor-thin

162

straight wings.

The speed of sound varies with both altitude and temperature, so for practical purposes the speed of an aircraft flying close to or above the speed of sound is expressed as a factor of whatever the speed of sound happens to be in the ambient conditions. This factor is the Mach number and the XS-1 attained Mach 1.012, just 1.2 per cent above the speed of sound, although later versions of the X-1 family achieved up to Mach 2.5. The speed of sound is about 660 mph at 36,000 ft, and conventional subsonic airliners cruise at Mach 0.8–0.85.

A practical SST, however, was a long way beyond the XS-1. The little rocket aircraft burnt fuel so fast that its powered flight endurance was measured in seconds (even the later versions had enough fuel for only two-and-a-half-minutes) and it had to be dropped from a B-50 Super-fortress bomber before making a fast, climbing speed run and gliding to a landing.

above
British Airways Concorde at Dubai airport

opposite
The first aircraft to break the sound barrier in level flight was the Bell XS-1

By the time the Farnborough studies started, the first jet fighters capable of exceeding Mach 1 in level flight had been flying for about a year. Aircraft like the USAF's F-100 Super Sabre hammered through the sound barrier by spraying neat fuel into the tailpipes of their engines, a process known as afterburning, which boosted power by almost 50 per cent but used so much fuel that supersonic excursions were still limited to a few minutes. The main problem with supersonic flight is a basic change in the relationship of the air to a moving body when the speed of that body becomes higher than the speed at which shock waves (such as sound) can spread. Instead of flowing smoothly around the aircraft from nose to tail, the air forms patterns of shock waves which stream back from the nose and from the leading edges of the wing like the bow wave of a boat. These waves are so powerful that they can have annoying or even destructive effects ten miles below the aircraft: the notorious sonic "boom". Because so much energy goes into creating these waves, an SST needs far more power than a subsonic airliner to carry the same load.

Another problem is the heating caused by air friction at high speeds. Ordinary alloys tend to become brittle after a few hundred hours under stress at high temperatures. A Mach 2 supersonic airliner has to be made from special aluminium alloys, and it was realised by the early 1950s that new materials such as stainless steel or titanium would have to be used for any aircraft cruising at Mach 3. Heating brings other problems for an airliner: it is reasonably easy to put a bomber crew into a refrigerated compartment, but to do the same with 100 passengers is a completely different matter.

The first time the Farnborough scientists looked at the SST, they came up with an aircraft weighing more than 300,000 lb and carrying just 18 passengers from London to New York. This was clearly impractical, and the team decided to start all over again.

Sustained supersonic flight appeared to demand a wing that was shallow in relation to its chord, but this conflicted with the need for an efficient structure and the demands of fuel stowage. The solution – originated by German designer Alexander Lippisch during the Second World War – was a triangular "delta" wing, extending along most of the fuselage length and providing plenty of stowage space with a structure that was deep (and thus light) while being shallow in relation to the chord. Lippisch was

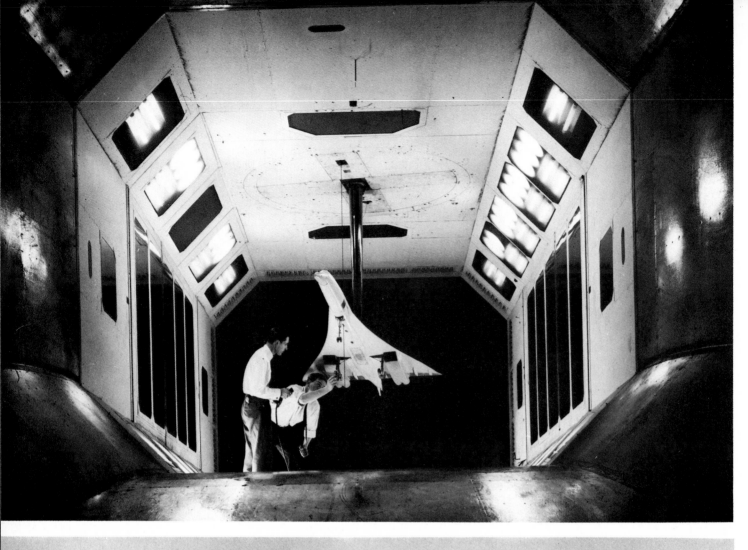

closely involved with the design of the supersonic Convair interceptors – the F-102 Delta Dagger and the F-106 Delta Dart – which led to the Mach 2 B-58 bomber. A similar delta planform was used in the British Fairey Delta Two, which brought the World Air Speed Record back to Britain in 1956. The delta was emerging as the best possible design for a Mach 2 SST; the RAE carried out extensive studies of a weird "M-wing" design to cruise at Mach 1.2, but this was not felt to be so attractive.

The British Ministry of Aviation, meanwhile, was beginning to feel that an SST could be a means of getting ahead of the US industry, which was just beginning to fly its first jet airliners. In November 1956, the Supersonic Transport Aircraft Committee (STAC) met for the first time, bringing together representatives from the aircraft and engine industries as well as the Farnborough scientists. Six days later, the Convair B-58 Hustler made its first flight; the American bomber was basically a subsonic-cruise design, and featured

an enormous, jettisonable fuel/weapon pod, but it was a step on the road to an SST.

The Bristol Aeroplane Company and the associated Bristol Engine Company showed most interest in the STAC proceedings, and these two manufacturers quickly moved to the forefront of British work on SSTs. The STAC had decided quite early in their deliberations to go for a 100-seat transatlantic SST flying just above Mach 2, the highest speed attainable without abandoning aluminium in favour of more exotic materials. The wing was to be a slim delta, swept at 70°.

By this time, however, airlines were beginning to be concerned about the long runways needed by their first-generation jets. The low-speed characteristics of the delta were quite unlike those of a conventional wing; it did not stall in the conventional way, but the nose could rise to a point where the wing was so inefficient that even full power could not stop the aircraft sinking towards the ground. The approach

opposite, top
The ogival wing of Concorde required extensive low-speed wind-tunnel testing

opposite, bottom
The subtle curves of the Concorde leading edge are accentuated in this view

below
A pre-production Concorde takes off on a test flight

167

The Concorde's Olympus engine was test flown under an Avro Vulcan bomber

and landing speeds of the Convair deltas were acceptable for military use, but not for the airlines. The solution lay with the discovery that a delta wing could be made to generate lift in a manner quite unlike the conventional wing, if the leading edge close to the root was swept sharply enough. A vortex would be created by the wing root and would spread along a carefully shaped leading edge, stabilising the airflow in much the same way as a leading-edge flap (although mechanical devices would not work on such a sharply swept wing). It was also found possible to reduce the sweep of the wing towards the tip without increasing the supersonic drag from shock waves or losing the vortex effect. The combination of sharper root sweep and a less sharply swept tip was blended into the compound-curved shape which medieval architects had christened the ogive. It was as aesthetically beautiful as it was aerodynamically elegant.

While the Bristol Aeroplane Company worked on the airframe, their colleagues in the Engine Company looked at the powerplant. The problem here was to drive an aircraft at Mach 2 without using reheat; what was needed was an engine which could produce a great deal of power by moving a relatively small mass of air at a very high speed. Bristol based their SST engine on the Olympus family, roughly equivalent to the Pratt & Whitney J57 and J75, but rather more powerful. They installed it behind a sophisticated variable intake that could take the Mach 2 airstream, slow it down and compress it before feeding it to the engine.

By 1961, Bristol had become the Filton Division of the British Aircraft Corporation and had the BAC 223 study on the drawing boards to meet the STAC specification. It had four Olympus engines of 30,000 lb-thrust and would weigh about 300,000 lb; the nose forward of the flight-deck

top
A "naked" Bristol Olympus turbojet
as fitted to the Avro Vulcan. Later
variants of the same engine were to
power Concorde

above
The Fairey FD.2 of the mid-1950s
was modified to become the BAC
221 test-bed for the Concorde's
ogival wing

left
Concorde's drooped nose originated
with the record-breaking Fairey
FD.2 supersonic research aircraft

169

was designed to droop for take-off and landing, a feature introduced on the Fairey Delta Two, so that the view from the flight-deck would be acceptable despite the high angle of attack on take-off and landing.

Meanwhile, the US manufacturers were studying supersonic-cruise aircraft on a military budget. In 1953, with the B-52 Stratofortress undergoing flight trials, the US Air Force issued study contracts for a supersonic replacement with a longer range than the B-58. The first studies of Weapon System 110A produced delta-wing, supersonic-dash vehicles which could cruise subsonically to the target with the aid of massive external tanks carried on jettisonable auxiliary wings. The USAF told the manufacturers to try again ("That's not an airplane, that's a three-plane

formation," exploded one USAF officer) and the manufacturers started working on aircraft which would cruise supersonically using special, boron-based fuels. In December 1957, North American beat Boeing in the WS-110A contest, and were awarded a contract to develop the Mach 3 B-70 Valkyrie bomber. The wing was to be a plain delta, manufactured from stainless-steel honeycomb, and the six engines occupied a massive wedge-shaped box beneath the wing. At Mach 3, the Valkyrie was expected to ride on the shock waves generated by the prow of this box and by the outer wing panels, which were designed to fold downwards through 65° at high speed. Each of the moving panels was almost as big as a B-58 wing. Rather than using the sophisticated

above
One of the forerunners of Concorde was Dassault's immensely successful Mirage fighter

opposite
Even heavier than Concorde, the massive North American B-70 Valkyrie Mach 3 bomber encouraged the USA to go for Mach 2.7 performance in an SST

Boeing proposed this variable-sweep aircraft as a Mach 2.7 SST. The engines were later moved beneath the tailplane, and the design was modified with a fixed wing before being cancelled. This, of course, is only a small-scale model

Farnborough aerodynamics, the B-70 had a large canard foreplane to lift the nose for take-off and landing.

Winning WS-110A clearly put North American in an excellent position to build an American SST if such a requirement should arise, and Douglas, Lockheed, Convair and Boeing all set up SST design teams to offset the North American

lead. In November 1959, the US Air Force cancelled the B-70 weapon system, but kept the prototype programme, partly because of Congressional fears that the Europeans – or even the Soviet Union – might beat the USA in the SST race. After a long and troubled development, the XB-70 flew in September 1964, but in two years of flight testing it never demonstrated its design range of

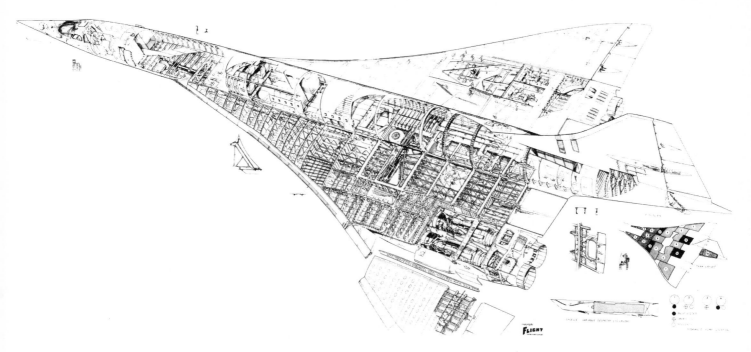

7,600 miles, and the compression-lift theory was quietly forgotten.

Meanwhile, Boeing had decided that an "arrowhead" planform would be more efficient than the delta; the main drawback was that the low-speed behaviour of a 70° swept wing was simply appalling. Boeing held an internal contest at the end of 1959 between a delta and a swept-wing design in which the wings could be swung forward for take-off and landing. The swing-wing design came out on top, but Boeing wisely decided to keep a delta programme running in parallel, in case the problems of variable-sweep became insuperable, The other US manufacturers backed the delta, with or without canards; Convair proposed a 60 seater with the B-58 wing.

The SST had not been so extensively studied in France as in Britain, but the French industry had amassed an impressive total of supersonic flying time by 1961, most of it on deltas, and they had the Mirage IV supersonic bomber under development. Sud-Aviation and Dassault – manufacturers of the Mirage family – had access to some British STAC material and decided to work together on an SST. In June 1961, they displayed a model of their Super-Caravelle project at the Paris air show. It looked very like the BAC 223, with four Olympus engines in paired nacelles under an ogival wing, but was designed for medium-range

rather than intercontinental routes. The rest of 1961 and most of 1962 were devoted to diplomatic manoeuvring and negotiations. Overshadowing everything else in Anglo-French relations was the question of British entry to the Common Market, and the possibility of a joint Anglo-French SST programme became a political pawn. The delicacy of relations between the two countries, combined with the fact that the SST was their first major collaborative programme, produced a number of compromises which were later to have an adverse effect on the development time and cost. Neither partner had design leadership or ultimate authority over the other, and technical decisions often had to be hammered out in committee; this sometimes produced solutions which combined the best of both countries' knowledge, but more often it produced delay. It was also decided that there were to be two production lines and, above all, that there was to be no "break clause" in the agreement.

By September 1962, BAC and Sud-Aviation (Dassault had dropped out) had a joint design to display at the Farnborough air show. There were two versions: a 100-seat, medium-range French aircraft and an 80-seat long-range aircraft which was to be a British responsibility. The Anglo-French agreement to work together on a supersonic transport was signed in late November 1962.

Some idea of the complicated structure of a modern jet airliner can be seen in this cutaway of Concorde. Note the complex fuel tank system shown at bottom right.

Six weeks later, President de Gaulle vetoed Britain's application to join the Common Market, christened the joint SST Concorde and stressed that it was a vital indicator of Britain's good faith in Europe. (The British called the aeroplane "Concord" without the final "e", for nearly five years, before conceding this "vital" point.)

It was hoped to have the aircraft in service by 1968, but the manufacturers had not taken full account of the time and cost (the two tend to amount to the same thing) involved in developing such a radically new aircraft to the standards of safety, reliability and profitability necessary for commercial service. And their schedule did not allow for anything going wrong. The SST was uniquely intolerant of performance shortfalls; unlike a military aircraft, it could not be put into service and corrected later, because safety could not be compromised, while its payload represented so small a fraction of its all-up weight that even a small overrun in structure weight or fuel consumption could render the aircraft useless.

The first major change to the Concorde project happened in the autumn of 1963, when the French finally accepted that the sonic "boom" would be intolerable over land, and that the medium-range Concorde was impractical. In late 1962, the US Government had run a series of "boom" tests over Oklahoma City, whose residents let it be known in no uncertain terms that sonic "boom" was not something communities could live with. By the end of 1963, therefore, Concorde had been scaled up into a transatlantic aircraft with a 118-seat cabin, and this standard was adopted for the two prototypes, the French-built 001 and the Filton-built 002. Maximum take-off weight rose to 326,000 lb.

The apparently rapid progress made by the British and French alarmed the Americans. The Federal Aviation Administration had been funding SST studies on a small scale since 1961, but – after the heavy losses which the US manufacturers had experienced on the big jets – the manufacturers were united in their unwillingness to take on develop-ment of the SST as a private venture. The alternative seemed to be government funding of an SST programme via the FAA, but free-enterprise enthusiasts condemned such a method as socialistic and un-American. Then, on June 4, 1963, Pan American took options on six Concordes. The next day, President Kennedy strongly backed the development of an SST with government funding. By August, the FAA had the authorisation to proceed, and asked for proposals from manufacturers. The US SST was to be bigger and faster than Concorde, with a speed of the order of Mach 3.

Of the three airframe proposals submitted in early 1964, North American's NAC-60 canard was rejected in the first round. Boeing conducted a new study into the merits of variable sweep compared with the delta, and decided once again that the swing-wing layout was superior. Its Model 733 proposal was a 435,000 lb, 165-seat aircraft cruising at Mach 2.7, rather slower than its rivals. The four engines were slung in individual pods beneath the fixed centre-section of the wing. Lockheed's L-2000 resembled Concorde most closely, with a double-delta wing and the engines mounted closely beneath the trailing edge. The FAA ran a parallel powerplant competition between Pratt & Whitney's JTF17A, a duct-burning turbofan, and General Electric's pure-jet GE4. Both engines were expected to yield up to 65,000 lb-thrust or even more.

One of the more ironic aspects of the competition was that Lockheed were already flying the world's most advanced supersonic aircraft when the FAA issued its request for proposals, but the team working on the L-2000 SST project knew nothing about it. Neither, in all probability, did the FAA. Development of the Lockheed A-11, a Mach 3.5 spy-plane with a range of well over 4,000 miles, had been ordered in 1958 by the US Central Intelligence Agency. Design and construction took place in Lockheed's Burbank "Skunk Works", staffed with hand-picked, security-vetted workers, and not one word leaked out until President Johnson revealed its existence in

March 1964. From that time on-wards, the Boeing and Lockheed teams were allowed limited access to the secrets of the A-11 (or SR-71 Blackbird, as production models are known), including its all-titanium structure and, in particular, its highly advanced variable air intakes. Lockheed were convinced that Boeing's ambitious, swing-wing design would not work, and felt that experience in building supersonic aircraft (which Boeing lacked) gave them a head start. Meanwhile, Boeing were promising great things from their tremendously complicated variable sweep design, including subsonic-quality low-speed handling.

The contest dragged on for two years, and both SST designs grew into 300-ton giants measuring more than 250 ft from nose to tail. Boeing's Phase II-B proposal, revealed as a stupendous, 306 ft-long, full-scale mock-up in September 1966, abandoned the arrowhead wing in favour of a configuration in which the wings folded back to blend with a massive tailplane, under which nestled the engines. "I guess they had to put them there to keep them from burning the tail off," was a Lockheed comment. Boeing called their II-B "more difficult, but more rewarding" than the Lockheed project. A double-jointed droop nose completed the

The Mach 3.5 Lockheed SR-71 Blackbird, which gave that company much experience in supersonic flight. Despite such Lockheed military successes, however, the American supersonic transport contract went to Boeing and the whole project was scrapped in 1971

The Tu-144 prototype displayed inadequate performance, and a programme of major modifications was put in hand

"prehistoric-monster" look of the Boeing project, now redesignated 2707. To Lockheed's astonishment and disgust, Boeing won the SST competition in December 1966. General Electric were awarded the contract to build the powerplant.

Meanwhile, a third SST programme was well under way in the research and development facility of the Tupolev design bureau. As the originator of Russia's first jet transports and the Soviet Air Force's first supersonic bomber (the Tu-22 Blinder), the Tupolev bureau was the natural choice to develop a supersonic airliner. Like the United States, the USSR was determined not to be left behind in the SST race. Unlike the USA, however, the Soviet Union decided to develop an SST very similar to Concorde; so similar, in fact, that the Western press nick-

named it "Concordski" when it was shown in model form at the 1965 Paris Air Show. The Tu-144 had the save ogival wing as Concorde, although of less complex shape. The main external difference between the two aircraft lay in the arrangement of the engines and main undercarriage. While the Concorde engines were installed in two paired nacelles midway along the wing span, with the landing gear legs retracting inwards into the wings and centre-section, the Tu-144's powerplants were installed in a single, massive box, with the main gear retracting vertically into the wings on either side. The Tu-144 main bogies each carried twelve small wheels so that they could fit into the thin outer wings. More significant, however, was the Russian decision to fit Kuznetsov NK-144 turbofans

The crowded engine nacelles and the TRA afterburning/reversal nozzles of a production Concorde

to their SST instead of pure jets like the Concorde's Olympus 593s. The problem with a turbofan is that, without reheat, its exhaust is not fast enough to propel a supersonic aircraft. Military aircraft use afterburning to go supersonic, but they spend most of their time at subsonic speeds, where the turbofan is more efficient than the pure jet. Not only were the Tu-144 engines more bulky that those of the Concorde, but at supersonic speed, with reheat, they were far less efficient.

Concorde, having survived an attempt by the British Labour Government to cancel it in 1964, proceeded more or less smoothly. The first prototype was scheduled to fly in February 1968, but before that time the decision was taken to enlarge the aircraft once again, to improve its economics. The proto-types continued unchanged, but it was decided that the pre-production and subsequent aircraft would be nine feet longer, with a new nose and slightly extended wings. Take-off weight grew towards 390,000 lb. In order to accommodate the greater weight in the same basic structure, the normal cruising speed was reduced from Mach 2.2 to Mach 2.05; this reduced the maximum temperature at which the structure would have to operate and permitted the guaranteed structure life to be maintained at the higher weights. At the same time, a partial reheat system was introduced on the Olympus engines, to cope with the higher weights on take-off and transonic acceleration. Inevitably, the decision to go for a bigger production aircraft caused the scheduled date of service to slip, and the costs to rise again.

Restricted by the small diameter of the Concorde fuselage, the complexity of the aircraft nevertheless means a vast number of instruments on the flight deck

Concorde's troubles were nothing, however, compared with those afflicting the Boeing 2707. In the course of 1967, it became clear that even Boeing had bitten off more than they could chew. Some airline pilots, meanwhile, were voicing concern about an aircraft with no fewer than 59 moving control surfaces. Soon after the 2707 won the FAA competition, it transpired that the aircraft was not only severely overweight, but would experience severe difficulty in flying at all, because of the short distance between the elevators and the centre of gravity. A small canard foreplane was added to lift the nose for take-off, solving the immediate problem but adding to the weight, which was now 75,000 lb over the target of 675,000 lb. In the spring of 1967, the wings were found to be too flexible, creating a stability problem. Stiffer wings meant yet more weight. Boeing managed to trim the weight down slightly, but were still far from producing a workable aircraft, and the FAA insisted that the first 2707 to fly had to be a workable airliner.

In 1968, as Boeing desperately tried to get the 2707 working,

Concorde 001 started taxi trials, but immediately ran into a series of minor problems with its brakes and landing gear. At the end of the year, on December 31, the Tu-144 became the first SST to fly. In the same month, Boeing finally admitted defeat with the swing-wing and revealed the 2707-300, with a broad, double-delta wing and a conventional tailplane; even to bring this aircraft to production specification would have cost several billion dollars.

Concordes 001 and 002 started their flight trials in March and April

1969, but considerable opposition to the SST projects was already building up on both sides of the Atlantic. Aircraft noise, scarcely an issue when the aircraft were conceived, had become a major problem, and critics said that it was nonsense to introduce aircraft noisier than the current generation and far outside the standards demanded of new, subsonic aircraft. With the development of the Boeing 747, it had become clear that the airline industry was taking a different direction from that envisaged when the SST projects were launched, and other critics ques-

tioned whether an SST would ever make money for the airlines, whatever the price. (With Concorde costs rising to almost three times the original estimates, the British and French Governments were fast resigning all hope of recovering their investments.) Worse still was the threat of high-altitude atmospheric pollution, which some people felt could create a permanent, high-level cloud layer.

The backbone of the US anti-SST lobby consisted of free-enterprise hard-liners who objected to a US Government subsidy for a commercial airliner programme; they were led by veteran campaigner Senator

William Proxmire of Wisconsin. In May 1971, faced with a Congressional refusal to grant any more money for the development of the Boeing SST, the US Administration cancelled the project. The SST programme had got to the engineering mock-up stage at a total cost ($980 million), nearly as high as the British or French share of Concorde (including all research and developmental costs, flight-testing and tooling) and rather more than Boeing spent on the entire development of the 747.

Public opposition, however, failed to break the French Government's commitment to Concorde, and the

above
Production-type Tu-144, showing the paired engines and retractable foreplanes. This photograph was taken at the 1973 Paris Air Show; minutes later, the aircraft broke up in flight

opposite
The Concorde prototypes continued to draw air show crowds (this one is at Farnborough) throughout the long development programme

The production version of the
Tu-144 featured a new engine
arrangement and retractable canard
foreplanes

182

A British Airways Concorde at
London Heathrow

British Government was unwilling
to offend the French by pulling out
of the project. In 1971, when the
first pre-production aircraft, 01, took
to the air, it was hoped to start
commercial services in 1974; the
fourth Concorde to fly, 02, was rolled
out in the following year and
featured a longer, more pointed tail-
cone representative of the production
aircraft. These two pre-series Concordes embarked on a long series of
flights to check whether the production aircraft could perform in accordance with specifications.

Environmental protest groups
were one thing the Soviet Union did
not have to worry about, but Tupolev had quite enough problems
without them. As might have been
expected, given its unsuitable powerplants, the Tu-144 was grievously
lacking in range, and it is probable
that a complete redesign was initiated
before the first aircraft flew, with the

first revised Tu-144 probably taking
to the air in mid-1972. The new
aircraft was 20 ft longer than the
prototype and considerably heavier,
carrying at least 40,000 lb more
fuel. The engines were installed in
paired pods rather than a single box,
and a completely new main landing
gear retracted into the pods, between
each pair of engines. The intakes
were redesigned – the prototype's
intakes had been strongly reminiscent of those of the Mikoyan MiG-25
fighter, but had presumably not been
efficient enough for an SST. The
most striking novelty, however, was
the installation of small, retractable
canard surfaces just behind the
flight-deck. Known as "mous-
taches", these had been tested by
Dassault on a Mirage in 1971. Their
function on a tail-less delta such as
the Tu-144 is to provide upwards
trim forces to raise the nose on take-
off; otherwise this has to be done by

upward deflection of the trailing-edge surfaces, subtracting from the total lift. On the Tu-144, they allowed the maximum take-off weight to be increased without causing an astronomical increase in take-off and landing runs.

The year 1973 was a bad one for SSTs. Flight trials of Concordes 01 and 02 revealed serious problems with the sophisticated variable inlets, and the 1974 in-service date drifted out of reach. Then, in June, one of the first production Tu-144s broke up in flight, following a structural overload while being demonstrated at the Paris air show. Meanwhile, Concorde's manufacturers had signed ten-year option agreements with many of the world's airlines in 1963; starting with Pan Am and TWA, most of them announced in 1973 that they would not be seeking to renew their commitments. Finally, in October came the Arab-Israeli war and a vast increase in fuel prices, making Concorde's economics even more of a problem. The following year, the British and French Governments decided that they would build no more Concordes after the batch of 16 production aircraft already approved, unless more aircraft were ordered. Air France and British Airways had ordered a total of nine Concordes in 1972, but both airlines stipulated that they had to be covered against any financial losses while operating those aircraft.

In 1975, Concorde completed an exhaustive series of endurance trials before being cleared to enter service at the end of the year. However, a new problem emerged when British Airways and Air France sought US permission to operate Concorde into New York and Washington. Stong local opposition, mainly on noise grounds, persuaded the US Government to make an intensive study of Con-

Production Concorde forward fuselages ready for delivery to the assembly line. Two final assembly lines were set up, one at Bristol and one at Toulouse

An unusual view of the third production Concorde, showing the distinctive paired engines

corde's effect on airport environment. The study concluded that the aircraft was acceptable, and operations into Washington started in May 1976 (the first Concorde services had been started to Rio de Janeiro and Bahrain in January). Local interests in New York, however, succeeded – through a string of court actions – in delaying the start of services on the premier Paris/London–New York transatlantic route until late 1977.

Well before that time, probably in early 1976, the Soviet Union concluded that the payload-range difficulties being experienced with the Tu-144 were insoluble, and production stopped with about ten aircraft completed. The Tu-144s operated an experimental service carrying a little freight from Moscow to Alma Ata, a distance of 2,000 miles, starting in November 1976; a year later, a weekly passenger service was inaugurated over the same route. Following an accident to one of the aircraft, however, the service was suspended in June 1978. At the time of writing there was no sign that services would restart.

Of the three contenders in the supersonic race, then, only Concorde has survived to operate effectively in service. The last of the 16 production aircraft was completed during 1979, and the total cost of the programme to the British and French Governments has been something in the region of £1,500 million. No further Concordes are likely to be built: commercially at least, the first generation of SSTs has been stillborn.

Jumbo

About the time that the airlines were buying their first fleets of long-range jet airliners, a British aviation commentator published a book called *An Industry Gone Mad*. The book argued that the move into jets was a suicidal extravagance on the part of the impoverished airlines, that the bigger, faster jets would produce a vast surplus of capacity and that the extra speed would not prove to be significant on the market.

The first half of the 1960s proved the commentator wrong, but events also surprised the official forecasters in the aviation industry itself. It was expected that the jets would be superseded by aircraft offering yet another increase in speed, at least on the longer routes; nearly all the research and development efforts directed towards commercial aircraft in the 1960–64 period went into supersonic airliners.

By 1964, however, there were signs that the airline industry was taking a wholly unexpected direction. By that time, the world's airlines had only recently taken delivery of the definitive long-range jets, the DC-8-50 and 707-320B/C, and were still adding these to their fleets at a fairly rapid pace. The earlier jets were well established on the US domestic scene, although the short-haul 727 was only just entering service. Jet travel had arrived, and was proving far more attractive than propeller travel. Combined with a boom in the Western economies and the fact that a jet seat-mile was actually turning out cheaper than a piston seat-mile, air fares started to lag behind inflation. In the mid-1960s, therefore, the air transport industry, led by the North Atlantic carriers and the US domestic trunk airlines, entered a period of sustained growth at over ten per cent a year. In many markets, 16 per cent growth was the norm. The airlines were faced with the prospect of doubling the size of their fleets every five years.

Expansion in the airline industry, however, did not please everybody. With increasing numbers of jet aircraft, the problems of noise and congestion began to loom as never before.

Aircraft noise had been recognised as a problem in some areas since the mid-1950s. In 1956, the transatlantic airlines introduced their first non-stop intercontinental Super Constellations and DC-7Cs on the London–New York route. Fully laden for the 3,500-mile flight, they staggered out of New York's Idlewild Airport (renamed John F. Kennedy International Airport in 1963) with their turbo-compound engines going full blast. The local residents decided that enough was enough, and persuaded the Port of New York Authority to apply the first-ever, statutory aircraft noise limit to all aircraft using Idlewild. Monitoring points were set up around the airport to ensure that no aircraft produced more than 112 decibels while more than a certain distance from the airport perimeter. Similar noise restrictions, based on the noise levels produced by the transatlantic piston types, were enforced at many other airports. The early jets, such as the Comet 4 and the pure-jet 707s and DC-8s, were fitted with simple "chute" silencers which reduced noise by smoothing out the mixing of the jet exhaust with the slipstream, although with a slight thrust loss. The JT3D-powered versions, with the slower exhaust velocity of the bypass engine, could meet the noise limits without silencers. The growth of the airline industry and the far wider use of jets in the early 1960s coincided with the expansion of residential communities around airports such as Idlewild, which had been a piece of marshy wasteland before it opened in 1946. Aircraft noise had become an explosive, potentially violent, political issue.

The noise problem contributed to another difficulty: the increasing congestion at the world's airports. The airline industry was expanding massively and the world's airports could not keep pace. Meanwhile, every plan for a new airport (such as the British project for a new international London airport at Stansted) was vigorously opposed by most local people. Nor could the air traffic control systems keep up with the air transport explosion: in the USA, it became commonplace for aircraft to be "stacked," flying in wide, descending spiral patterns while waiting for permission to land. Often, they used up so much fuel in the stack that they were forced to divert to an airport less crowded than their destination. The sheer number of aircraft in the air was beginning to make mid-air collisions an ever-present risk, as clearances between aircraft were reduced in an effort to clear the blockages.

Airline executives do a great deal of flying in the course of their business and, inevitably, many of them found themselves caught in the massive aerial traffic jams around the major airports. The answer to the congestion problem, so firmly brought home to the airline chiefs, was so simple that it germinated in the minds of most of the world's airlines at about the same time, in early 1965: fewer, bigger aircraft. In fact, with double-figure traffic growth, much bigger aircraft.

Just as military developments had provided the technology for the first-generation jets, so a US Air Force requirement produced the solution

The first prototype 747 was retained by Boeing for test flying, including trials with General Electric CF6 engines

to this problem before the airlines realised they had one.

Since the end of the Second World War, Western military strategy had tended to rely increasingly on rapid reinforcement of NATO military forces in Europe by troops and equipment from the USA. The world's largest transport aircraft, with the sole exception of the Tu-114 Cleat, had consistently been those flying with the US Air Force Military Air Transport Service (MATS): the Douglas Globemaster I and II, and the pressurised, turboprop C-133 Cargomaster. But MATS had always looked for an aircraft even bigger and heavier than these. The monstrous Douglas C-132 got to the mock-up stage in 1957, but was cancelled; it would have had swept wings and four, 15,000 ehp turboprops, like the Tu-114, and would have weighed some 225 tons. But the requirement remained, and was only partly met by the Lockheed C-141 StarLifter, a military freighter slightly bigger than a 707. By the time the C-141 flew in December 1963, the US airframe manufacturers were working on the USAF's CX-4 requirement for a strategic freighter capable of moving the heaviest items of military equipment, and the engine manufacturers were designing its powerplant under the US Air Force's STF-200 demonstrator programme. The USAF had decided that the right engine for a super-heavy freighter was the high-bypass-ratio turbofan. In a low-bypass engine such as the JT3D, roughly as much air passes through the compressor, combustion chamber and turbine as flows through the fan; in a high-bypass-ratio engine, anything up to six times as much air flows through the fan. The engine is more efficient at subsonic speeds than the low-bypass engine, but is vastly more difficult technically because of the enormous tensile stresses on the fan blades and the need for an extremely high pressure ratio in the core (the compressor and turbine) of the engine. Unless the core runs at a high pressure ratio, the big fan will not spin fast enough to operate efficiently at speeds up to Mach 0.9.

Pratt & Whitney and General Electric ran static demonstrator engines as part of the STF-200 programme; in Britain, Rolls-Royce had been thinking along very similar lines since the early 1960s, reasoning that the high-bypass-ratio engine would be the natural powerplant for the next generation of airliners, and they were working on an engine known as the RB.178 Super Conway, although any resemblance to the earlier engine disappeared at an early stage in the programme.

The new generation engines were offering nearly 40,000 lb-thrust, but – because the exhaust was slower – the mixing process with the outside air was much more gentle than in earlier aircraft engines, and large aircraft with the new engines would therefore be little noisier than the smaller aircraft already in service in 1964.

The continuing improvements in aerofoil technology, and the improvement in high-lift systems evidenced by the 727 and the DC-9-30, were promising more efficient airframes for the new generation. The new aircraft would be lighter per passenger seat than the older types, and the new engines would burn up to 25 per cent less fuel per pound of thrust. Newer, larger aircraft would not only ease the aircraft congestion at airports and bring the noise nuisance under control, they would also be much cheaper per seat-mile.

In September 1965, Lockheed won the competition to build the big freighter for the US Air Force, designated C-5A Galaxy; Boeing and Douglas, their two rivals for the contract, transferred their C-5A design teams to big-airliner study programmes. GE won the contract for the USAF engine, which was to be a 39,000 lb-thrust engine with a 6:1 bypass ratio, designated TF39. Like Boeing and Douglas, Pratt &

Whitney diverted their big-fan efforts to civil projects.

The need for bigger aircraft was urgent, however, and the new generation of aircraft would not be ready for several years. Douglas and Boeing both saw the opportunity to stretch existing aircraft, adding a great deal of capacity without adding much to operating costs. The economics of this process were very attractive; the airlines could add up to 50 revenue seats virtually free of charge, and the seat-mile costs tumbled. The stretched aircraft could be flown and overhauled with the minimum of new training or equipment, so the introduction costs were kept low.

The first of the "stretches" to appear was the Douglas DC-8-61, starting the Super 60 series of DC-8 developments. It was no less than 37 ft longer than the DC-8-50, but used the same wing and engines; it could seat up to 261 passengers in a high-density layout. The drawback was that it had less range than the intercontinental-50, being optimised for high-density US domestic routes. Nearly all of the DC-8-61s sold went to US trunk airlines, United and Eastern being among the first major customers. Freighter and convertible versions were also developed. The DC-8-61 flew in 1965, but it was only the first of a family of stretched DC-8s. The next version to fly was the DC-8-62; only eight feet longer than the -50, it had more powerful engines, modified nacelles and pylons, extended low-drag wingtips and a longer range than any other jet until the appearance of the 747SP in the mid-1970s. It was bought by a number of airlines for specialised, long-haul operations, but was only a step on the way to the ultimate DC-8, the -63 version. This combined the -61 fuselage with the wing and engines of the long-range -62, producing a 250-seater with the intercontinental range of the DC-8-50 and the lowest seat-mile costs of any long-range aircraft at the time. The Super 63 had an impact on the air transport scene out of all proportion to the relatively small number built; by the time the type entered service, most of the world's airlines were already committed to the new generation aircraft. Many of the stretched DC-8s were bought by the US "supplemental" (or charter) airlines, which at that time were growing rich ferrying US military personnel and cargo to and from the war in South-East Asia. With the end of US involvement in Vietnam in the early 1970s, the charter operators switched to the North Atlantic market, and it was largely their competition, using the highly economical Super DC-8s, that brought about the decline in average air fares during the first half of the 1970s. The freighter and convertible Super DC-8s also became the mainstay of the cargo airlines.

The classic stretch, however, was Boeing's 727-200, which emerged rather later than the first Super DC-8s and entered service in 1967. It was 20 ft longer than the original 727, and over short sectors could carry as many passengers as a 707-320. The original versions could not match the 727-100 in range, which limited the market, but in 1971 Boeing introduced the heavier, more powerful, Advanced 727-200. This aircraft superseded the much less economical 727-100 on the production line, and was still the world's best-selling airliner in 1976. Later 727-200s had sound-absorbent material added to their engine nacelles, enabling them to meet new noise rules; 727s sold in the USA after 1973 were limited in gross weight by those noise rules, but aircraft delivered to foreign airlines weighed up to 209,000 lb and could carry 189 passengers more than 2,000 miles. Later 727s were powered by improved JT8Ds of up to 17,400 lb-thrust.

The final phase of the European war between the 727 and Trident,

top
The DC-8-61, 37 ft longer than the standard aircraft, was developed to meet the vast increase in traffic on US domestic routes in the mid-1960s

above
This unusual air-to-air photograph shows the clean lines of the original DC-8 jet transport

broke out in 1967, when British European Airways decided that they wanted to buy 727-200s. BEA, as related earlier, had insisted nine years before that the Trident should be scaled down, but they now decided that it was too small. Finally, the British airline was forced to order a stretched Trident, the 3B, with a small, RB.162 booster jet in the tail, but the compromise was an unhappy one and only 28 Trident 3Bs were sold. The only major export customer for the Trident was China, where US manufacturers were not allowed to sell aircraft until the mid-1970s. The Trident production line finally closed down in 1978, after 117 aircraft had been built; by that time, Boeing had sold over 1,500 727s and were still building them at a rate of six aircraft a month. More than two-thirds of the 727s sold have been stretched 727-200s, and the type has sold to airlines in greater numbers

than any other airliner in history (allowing for the fact that nearly all the Douglas DC-3s were originally military aircraft).

Boeing's main reason for deciding in late 1965 to stretch the 727 was that, while they wanted to participate in the US domestic market, they were also after bigger game on the intercontinental scene. Like Douglas, Boeing looked hard at a stretched version of the 707, the 707-820; this might have been an even bigger aircraft than the DC-8-63, with Rolls-Royce RB.178s in one version. But the 707 had a shorter landing gear than the DC-8, and a new gear would have been necessary if the aircraft was to be stretched. This would have made the operation more expensive than the Super 60 programme, and by mid-1965 Boeing decided that the 707-820 was not worth the effort.

Meanwhile, all the US manufacturers involved in the C-5A contest

had looked at airliner versions of their submissions; these would have been enormous, high-wing designs carrying more than 800 passengers on two decks. By September 1965, however, Boeing had decided that this was the wrong way to go. Such an aircraft would carry too many passengers and did not offer enough range; the company had already rejected a high wing for airliner-use once, in 1946; and the C-5A studies were to be slower than the existing jets. Starting with a clean sheet of paper and four of the new, big-fan engines, however, offered a great many advantages.

By September 1965, the Boeing 747 was taking shape. The company decided to exploit new transonic

The workhorse of the US domestic network throughout the 1970s, the stretched 727-200 was another ''interim'' high-capacity aircraft built to meet 1960s traffic densities

aerofoil technology in the interests of higher speed, with cruise speeds of Mach 0.9 and more in prospect. To keep the wing small for fast, efficient cruise, the high-lift devices would be taken beyond the 727 stage: the wing trailing-edge would be fitted with sophisticated, triple-slotted flaps, while the sharp high-speed leading edge would carry elaborate, modified-Kruger flaps (fitted with a flexible lip) over the entire span. One very important move was the decision to go for a single passenger deck. In theory, two decks, as on the C-5A, would make more efficient use of the fuselage volume, which left a great deal of apparently wasted space above and below the passenger cabin. In practice, however, the single deck vastly simplified the construction of the

fuselage and allowed an egg-shaped cross-section, more aerodynamically efficient than the square section of the C-5A. Under the floor was a cavernous freight hold, designed to be filled with specially designed containers; above the passengers' heads, in space which might otherwise have been left unused, were deep, drop-down stowage bins for coats and baggage. The wide cabin could seat up to ten passengers abreast, although most early customers installed only nine seats across the economy-class cabin, with two aisles instead of one.

One of the later 747 decisions was the location of the flight deck. The problem was to give the pilots an adequate view to the sides and rear of the aircraft, despite the width of the body. Boeing's solution was to perch the flight-deck on top of the passenger cabin, leaving the fuselage nose clean, sharp-pointed and uncluttered. The flight-deck caused a drag problem until Boeing faired it more gently into the main body, creating the 747's characteristic upper passenger lounge. In a deliberate throwback to the Stratocruiser, Boeing installed a spiral staircase from the main cabin to the upstairs lounge.

Everything about the 747 broke new ground – from its four, independent hydraulic systems and its four main landing gear bogies, to the inertial navigation system, which used accelerometers mounted on a gyro-stabilised platform and linked to a computer to give the aircraft's exact position at any time, independent of all radio aids. (Like the Trident's automatic landing system, this had to be fully triplicated so that two correct systems could "vote down" a faulty third platform.)

The initial, transatlantic 747-100 was expected to weigh no less than 690,000 lb, just over twice as much as the 707-320B, but its 236 ft-long fuselage could seat up to 490 passengers, two-and-a-half times the capacity of the older jet: now classified as a "narrow-body" airliner. The weight and payload were not the only superlatives, however: the programme meant a research and development investment which was very nearly the total value of Boeing's assets (less their current debts). If the 747 flopped, it would almost certainly take Boeing with it.

One factor in Boeing's favour, however, was the financial position of Douglas, who were in deep trouble on their DC-9 production programme and certainly in no position to launch their own, four-jet widebody. If Boeing moved fast, therefore, there was a good chance that they could work up an unbeatable lead and have the top end of the market to themselves, avoiding the destructive competition which had characterised the DC-8/707 battle. In April 1966, Pan Am signed up for 25 Boeing 747s; the first aircraft was to fly at the end of 1968 and services were to begin at the start of 1970. During the rest of 1966, the world's

airlines fell over themselves in the rush to order 747s, and Douglas had to renounce any ambitions they had on the market. Even stalwart Douglas airlines like Alitalia and KLM had to buy 747s or risk being wiped out on the North Atlantic by Pan Am and TWA. Also a victim of the 747's advance was BAC's projected, stretched VC10, with two decks, 265 seats and Rolls-Royce RB.178s.

Pratt & Whitney's long experience with civil jet engines, and in particular their very successful JT3D and JT8D, were important factors in securing the contract to power Pan American's 747s and, indeed, every other aircraft of the type ordered over the next eight years. Pratt & Whitney's engine for the 747 was the JT9D, with a thrust of just over 40,000 lb in its initial version; by the time the 747 entered service, the standard engine was the 43,500 lb-thrust JT9D-3A.

Rolls-Royce were proposing their massive RB.207 for the 747, starting at 47,500 lb-thrust and with growth potential well beyond this; they were also working on the smaller, RB.211, rated in early 1966 at about 33,000 lb-thrust. Both the Rolls-Royce engines had three concentric shafts, in contrast to the two-shaft layout favoured by the US manufacturers. The three-shaft layout made the engine more complex in some respects, and tended to increase its weight, but the Rolls-Royce engines were shorter than those of their US rivals. The British company hoped that the shorter shafts would be stiffer, that the tolerances within the engines would be tighter and that their engines would thus be more efficient than the two-shaft types.

Pratt & Whitney were concerned that the RB.207 might be applied to the proposed European twin and to European airlines' 747s. By 1967, it was clear that many of the 747s sold would be longer-range, 775,000 lb 747-200s (or 747Bs); Lufthansa, for example, decided to buy the heavier aircraft almost from the outset, despite the fact that other airlines would have their – 100s in service first. Pratt & Whitney had their· 46,500 lb-thrust JT9D-7 under de-

velopment for the 747-200, and were keen to keep their monopoly on the 747. They proposed a collaborative agreement with Bristol Siddeley in the UK and Snecma in France to develop and manufacture the JT9D, but the plan was foiled by Rolls-Royce's takeover of Bristol Siddeley in 1967.

Meanwhile General Electric had decided that the TF39, as fitted to the C-5A, was not ideal for the civil market, and they decided to apply their TF39 knowledge more generally to a new civil turbofan in the same category as the RB.211. Both

the new GE project, designated CF6, and the RB.211 were aimed at the same market, the outlines of which had started to become clear in early 1966. In February of that year, American Airlines' chief engineer Frank Kolk was caught in the New York "stack" after a visit to General Electric, where he had been briefed on progress with the TF39 engine. The delay started him thinking, and – the next day – American issued a one-page request for proposals covering a short-haul, wide-body transport. It would have two engines, 250 seats and a range of

above
A Boeing 747 in the colours of TWA, one of the world's largest operators of the type

opposite, top
The upper deck of a 747 was a return to the days of the Stratocruiser. Later, as low fares spread, some airlines removed the lounge and installed high-density seating

opposite, bottom
The enormous complexity of the big-fan engines is well shown in this view of a Pratt & Whitney JT9D, capable of delivering 53,000 lb-thrust

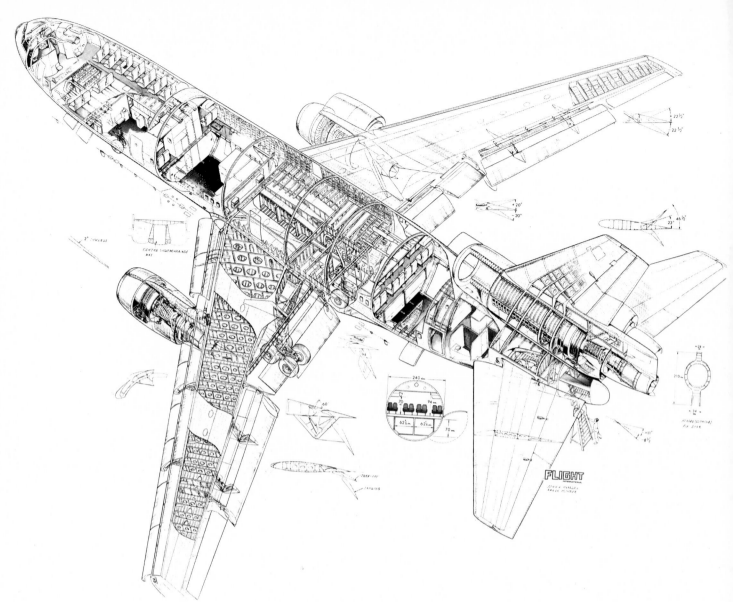

Cutaway drawing of the McDonnell Douglas DC-10-30, with its twin-wheel auxiliary landing gear

about 1,500 miles. Unlike the 747, then two months away from a launch decision, it would be able to operate efficiently from runways shorter than 8,000 ft.

It was not American's fault that it was to be 12 years before any US airline bought an aircraft corresponding even roughly to the "Kolk machine". The airline's thinking corresponded closely to French ideas for what was called the "airbus", a large-capacity twin designed for short range and minimum cost. Such an aircraft, the HBN.100 Galion, had been studied by a consortium of French manufacturers as early as 1965, and by 1966 the concept was attracting the interest of Hawker Siddeley's Hatfield division (formerly de Havilland). It seemed ideal for short, dense European routes.

Of the US manufacturers in the airliner business when American

Airlines issued their draft proposal, Boeing were totally involved with the 747, Douglas were having financial problems and Lockheed were busy with defence contracts and the L-2000 SST. Both Douglas and Lockheed produced designs for a big twin; however, it was not until the end of the year that either company was in a position to conduct serious studies. In December 1966, Lockheed lost the SST contest to Boeing, and Douglas were taken over by McDonnell. One of the first decisions made by McDonnell when it took over was that Douglas had to have a wide-body in the market, at whatever cost.

Throughout the first half of 1967, Lockheed and Douglas were chasing the same customers, with aircraft that would use the same engines and would be developed to a similar timetable. TWA, United, American and

Eastern were the main targets, and if either manufacturer could land three of them there was a good chance that the rival would drop out.

Once again, United Airlines insisted that no twin-engined aircraft could meet their inflexible requirement for operations out of the high-level airport at Denver. United wanted their aircraft to take off from Denver with a full payload and carry it to the East Coast (a distance of over 2,000 miles) or to the West Coast over the Rocky Mountains, a tough requirement in terms of engine-out cruise altitude. By September 1967, the two manufacturers in the hunt had accepted that the aircraft would have to be a trijet; at that time about 37,000 lb of thrust was expected from the GE CF6 or the RB.211, while Pratt & Whitney had a scaled-down JT9D on offer, of about the same rating.

In February 1968, American Airlines placed the first order for a wide-body trijet, buying 25 McDonnell Douglas DC-10s. In the following month, TWA, Eastern and Delta chose the Lockheed L-1011, later named the TriStar. For a month, the future of the DC-10 hung in the balance, because it was possible that McDonnell Douglas would not go ahead if United also bought TriStars; but in April, United announced that they would buy DC-10s. Not only would there be two, wide-body trijets, but they would be powered by different engines: Lockheed had decided that the TriStar would have RB.211s, while McDonnell Douglas chose the General Electric CF6 for their DC-10.

Under the circumstances, it was hardly surprising that the two trijets should be so similar; but that their

British Airways are so far the only airline to use Lockheed TriStars on European domestic services, having ordered the type in 1972

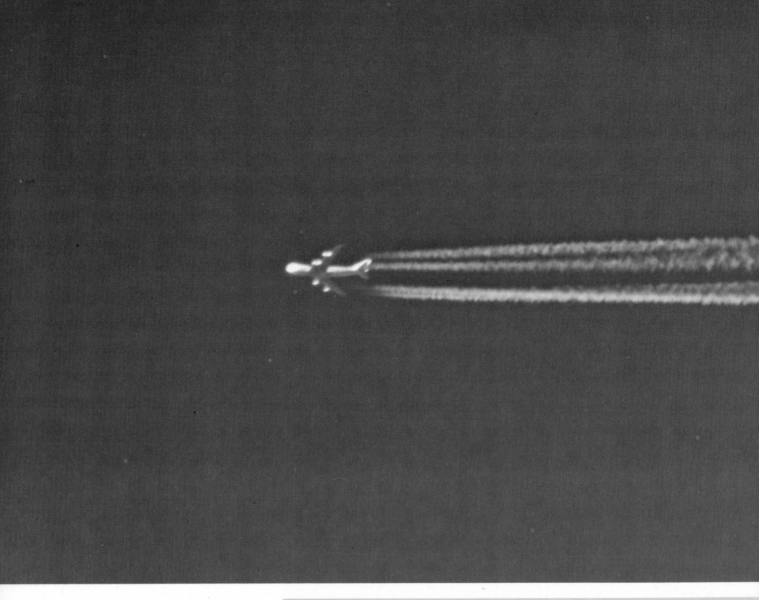

above
Boeing 747 contrailing at altitude
over London Heathrow Airport

right
DC-10 of Lufthansa

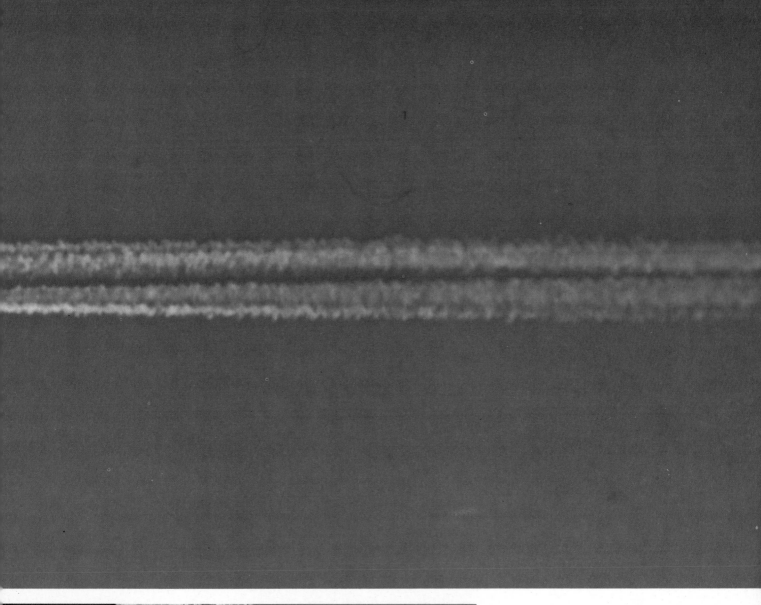

left
KLM were the first airline to order
Boeing 747s equipped with General
Electric CF6-50E turbofans

The long-haul DC-10-30 was
originally built for European
carriers such as Lufthansa

wing spans should be identical to
the inch (155 ft 4 in) seemed to be
carrying things a little too far. The
wings of both aircraft were swept at
35°, fractionally less than the 747
wing, and both carried double-
slotted, trailing-edge flaps and full-
span slats on the leading edge. Both
aircraft had circular-section fuselages, designed to seat eight passengers abreast in a comfortable US
layout, and both could carry about
260 mixed-class passengers (most US
airlines later converted their interiors to carry more passengers).
The freight holds of both types could
accept the special containers being
designed for the 747; some airlines,
feeling that they could not fill the
lower hold with freight, had lower-
deck galleys installed, making room
for more passengers on top. Both

trijets had conventional flight decks
in the nose, rather than 747-style
upper decks. Both aircraft had a
range of about 3,000 miles with a
full load of passengers, baggage and
freight.

The differences between the two
were also numerous, however, despite their basic similarity. The most
obvious was that the TriStar's third
engine was buried in the tail – like
that of the 727 – while that of the
DC-10 was carried on the tailfin in a
straight-through nacelle. This
avoided the complication of the S-
shaped intake duct on the TriStar,
but meant the installation of massive, banjo-shaped fin spars. Both
aircraft had two underwing engines
and one rear engine; the big-fan
powerplants were too large for efficient rear-fuselage mounting, and

the potential bending relief on the wing was vital on such large aircraft. The installation of the rear engine meant that the TriStar had a longer rudder than the DC-10, so that it was easier to control should the left or right engine be lost; thus Lockheed could hang their engines further outboard and fit an undercarriage of wider track than the DC-10's. The TriStar had a powered "flying tail" linked to the wing spoilers to provide very precise and immediate control of altitude on the approach, while the DC-10 had more conventional controls. The TriStar's flaps were extended along tracks, while those of the DC-10 swung out on simple pivots, carried below the wing in streamlined, fin-like fairings.

TriStar and DC-10 salesmen made 'a great deal of these points, but what

really made the difference in the commercial success of the two types during the early years of development was McDonnell Douglas's decision to develop a long-range version of the DC-10 at an early stage in the programme. One of the reasons why the US airlines were keen on a trijet was their belief that it could be an "all-purpose" aircraft, as economical on long routes as on short, high-frequency operations. McDonnell Douglas took the first key orders for long-haul aircraft in 1969: Northwest Airlines ordered the DC-10-20 (later redesignated the -40) with Pratt & Whitney JT9D-20s, while the European KSSU group, comprising SAS, KLM, Swissair and UTA, ordered DC-10-30s. The latter version, which took the vast majority of long-range

Modern airliners are designed to be flexible to ensure maximum commercial impact. Douglas have always been experts at this, and their latest products continue in the company tradition. The DC-9-20 (*top left*) was a special "hot rod" version for SAS; variants of the DC-10 include the -30CF convertible (*top right*) with its powered freight handling equipment; the JT9D engined -40 (*bottom left*); and the passenger-only -30 (*bottom right*). Note the central landing gear leg and the flexing of the wing under load on the latter example

Delta Air Lines were among the prime customers for the Lockheed TriStar at the time of its inception in 1968, putting the aircraft in service in 1972

DC-10 sales (only Japan Air Lines has followed Northwest in buying the -40), was powered by the General Electric CF6-50, a highly modified version of the CF6 fitted to the domestic aircraft. (The US domestic DC-10 became the DC-10-10, and its powerplant was the CF6-6.)

The new, CF6-50 offered 49,000 lb-thrust in its initial version with the prospect of more to come. The wingtips of the intercontinental DC-10 were extended by five feet each side to improve the take-off performance, and a twin-wheel auxiliary landing gear was added on the centreline to cater for the higher gross weight; the first intercontinental DC-10s took off at 555,000 lb. The fuel capacity was increased in proportion, and the DC-10-30 could carry a full load of passengers and baggage for up to 5,000 miles. For many airlines it was easier to make the step from narrow-bodies to the DC-10 than to jump straight up to the 747. The intercontinental DC-10 was soon selling faster than the domestic versions, which did not sell as well as the TriStar.

One casualty of the DC-10-30/40 programme was the DC-8-63F. The stretched narrow-body was simply too much of a rival to the wide-body, in which the company had invested so much money, and it was taken out of production in 1972 despite steady airline demand. By that time, 556 DC-8s had been sold. Six years later, the scarce and irreplaceable DC-8-63F freighters were still worth far more on the second-hand market than their original customers had paid for them.

Lockheed's first long-haul TriStar, the L-1011-8, was in many ways more advanced and more extensively modified from its domestic forebear than was the DC-10-30/40. It was shelved after the DC-10 pre-empted the market with the KSSU order.

General Electric's "growth" CF6-50 was aimed at another application beside the DC-10-30: the European project for a twin-engined wide-body. In July 1967, this became a joint Anglo-French-German effort, the A300 Airbus, and it was very nearly as large and as heavy as the

US trijets, with two of Rolls-Royce's vast RB.207 engines of 54,000 lb-thrust. In early 1969, the project was reviewed and the airframe partners decided that it should be made smaller to move it into a market slot of its own. Accordingly, it was scaled down to about 280 seats by European standards (240 American seats), becoming the A300B.

The smaller aircraft would work quite well with the JT9D-7, the CF6-50 or a more powerful RB.211. The British Government had been convinced by Rolls-Royce that engines were more important than airframes, and was mainly interested in the A300 as a vehicle for the RB.207, which seemed a promising powerplant for later 747s. In early 1969, the British Government withdrew from the A300 programme, although Hawker Siddeley remained involved as a subcontractor, with responsibility for the wings.

While the Europeans played politics, the Americans produced hardware. The first 747 flew at the beginning of 1969, and the type entered service on schedule a year

above
The first Boeing 747 was rolled out
at Everett in late 1968

right
The flight-deck of the 747 is
smaller than those of other wide-
bodies, being located in the
narrower upper deck of the aircraft

The operation of a 747's thrust reversers is checked out with a model in a smoke tunnel

later. The JT9D, however, suffered some very severe problems: the fan case was insufficiently rigid, and the engine was burning out turbine blades with monotonous regularity.

As Boeing and Pratt & Whitney struggled to get the 747 working reliably, a recession hit the airline industry. Airlines suddenly realised that they had been too hasty in buying 747s and delayed deliveries as far as possible. The flow of orders dried up completely in 1970 and 1971. With vast rows of undelivered 747s parked outside the massive new factory which Boeing had built to make the giant airliner, the Boeing balance sheet began to make depressing reading. Takeover or bankruptcy seemed a matter of months away. Boeing realised that they had gone too far in building up 747 production and the 747 workforce. Their first step was to reduce their outgoings by cutting the workforce by

nearly two-thirds – "Will the last one out of Seattle please turn out the lights?" was a common slogan. At the same time, the company decided that they had been neglecting the 727 and 737, and modified them with new interiors, higher gross weights, rough-runway kits and other options. The flow of orders for these established types started to increase, and Boeing concentrated on producing them in as few manhours as possible. By the time the slack in the 747 market had been taken up, Boeing had pulled through, but they were grimly determined not to repeat the mistake of over-reacting to a rising market.

Meanwhile, the British industry seemed to be dropping plans for large airliners. BAC had proposed their narrow-body, twin-RB.211, BAC Two-Eleven 200-seater to BEA in 1967, but (by 1969) the RB.211 had grown to more than 40,000 lb-

The operation of a 747's thrust reversers is checked out with a model in a smoke tunnel

thrust and the BAC project became a wide-bodied Three-Eleven, in the same class as the A300 but looking like an overgrown One-Eleven, with rear engines and a T-tail. BEA wanted the Three-Eleven, as did Laker Airways and a number of other carriers, and – in late 1969 – BAC asked for British Government launching aid, saying that it now had airline commitments for more than 40 aircraft. The powerplant would have been the uprated, 50,000 lb-thrust RB.211-61, and Rolls-Royce wanted launching aid for that as well.

The Three-Eleven, unfortunately, was overtaken by events. In June 1970, the Labour Government – which had been sympathetic to the project and seemed likely to give its blessing – was defeated in a General Election. By the time the Conservative Government under Edward Heath came to consider the aircraft and its engine, both the RB.211 and Rolls-Royce themselves were in serious trouble.

Rolls-Royce had planned to get ahead of their US rivals by making the fan of the RB.211 out of carbon fibre rather than titanium, achieving a substantial weight saving even in the context of an airliner the size of a TriStar. After the first field tests of carbon-fibre fans – on the engines of a BOAC VC10 – it became quite clear that the composite material could not stand up to the erosive

The first of the "jumbos" was the US Air Force's C-5A transport. Production losses on the vast freighter nearly drove Lockheed into bankruptcy. Four C-5As, two with flight-test probes, are seen at Marietta in the early stages of the programme

effects of rain or hail. The switch back to titanium meant that Rolls-Royce had to supply more power to offset the extra weight, and this added to a number of problems which were forcing the costs of the programme out of control, up to four times the original estimates. The company had signed a contract with Lockheed guaranteeing a fixed price

for every RB.211, so there seemed no way in which the massive cost over-run could be recovered. By the autumn of 1970, Rolls-Royce had asked the British Government to keep the company going. The Government had been elected on a platform of rigorous private enterprise, and the request for Three-Eleven and RB.211-61 money could

not have come at a worse time. It was rejected, together with a Hawker Siddeley proposal that Britain should rejoin the Airbus programme as a full partner. Finally, at the beginning of 1971, Rolls-Royce was told there would be no more Government money. The company had no choice but to declare themselves bankrupt. All the Rolls-Royce agreements with Lockheed became void, and the US company discovered that they were in the position of selling gliders. The configuration of the TriStar (which, like the DC-10, had made its first flight the previous autumn) made it highly expensive to change engines, and the delay would in any case be unacceptable to Lockheed's customers.

Throughout 1971 and part of 1972, Lockheed and the British Government negotiated a package agreement which would keep the

RB.211 programme going. Lockheed were in difficulties on their own account, having signed a fixed-price contract for C-5A development and then having incurred massive cost overruns; finally the company had to accept a "fixed loss" on each C-5A as part of their settlement with the Pentagon. Eventually, a new price was agreed for the RB.211 and Lockheed's survival was ensured by US Government-backed loans.

In the autumn of 1972, the two US domestic trijets went into service with their first US customers. Another development in that year was a British Airways order for the TriStar, confirming the links between the British industry and the US manufacturer. In the summer, the first A300 built by the Airbus Industrie consortium took off from Toulouse, into a sky which seemed very full of American aeroplanes.

Saudia were one of the main export customers for the TriStar and its Rolls-Royce engines

High industry

The early 1970s saw a major change in the airline industry and in the business of building commercial aircraft. The near-collapse of Douglas, Boeing and Lockheed in turn led to a much tougher attitude to the business of selling airliners, as it became clear that not even the largest company could survive another error such as General Dynamics/Convair had made in launching the 880/990 series. The stakes were simply too high: research, development and tooling for a new airliner could cost as much as an entire company was worth.

By the early years of the 1970s it also became clear that the industry had reached something of a "technology plateau," partly because the airliner designers had taken a different course from the military. Military research and development was no longer easily applicable to the design of airliners, and any major innovation in design would have to be carried on the budget of a commercial programme. As well as increasing the costs, any new and untried departure could spell catastrophe for a civil programme and its manufacturer if an unforeseen snag appeared at a late stage. Rolls-Royce had proved that with their attempt to develop a carbon-fibre fan for the RB.211 engine, and any airframe manufacturer could obviously go the same way.

By 1972, four major Western concerns were engaged in the development and production of wide-body airliners. Two of the US companies in the race were fairly similar: both McDonnell Douglas and Lockheed were predominantly defence contractors; the former were now run from the McDonnell headquarters at St Louis, more than a thousand miles from their commercial manufacturing centre, and the Douglas

division were carefully supervised by the almost entirely military contractor (McDonnell) which had taken them over. To put the airliner business into perspective, even a fighter like the F-15 Eagle – built by McDonnell Douglas at St Louis – can cost three-quarters as much as a DC-10 wide-body airliner. Lockheed had even more military business than McDonnell Douglas, but their misfortunes in military contracts had been as painful as the problems of the TriStar programme: the company had badly underestimated the costs of the C-5A Galaxy military freighter, and fatigue tests then revealed that the wing would only last some 7,000 hours in the air; the US Army's Cheyenne helicopter also had to be cancelled. Thus Lockheed did not suffer from the sort of tension that existed between the military and commercial divisions at McDonnell Douglas, where the military people felt that they were subsidising the commercial operations.

In sharp contrast, the third of the US manufacturers, based in Washington state rather than in sunny California, had a commitment to civil manufacture that was large and increasing, with the rundown of Minuteman ballistic missile production and of their other military programmes.

The recession of the early 1970s had taught Boeing the dangers of overreacting to the booms and slumps of the highly erratic airline industry. In the late 1960s, the airlines had seen strong growth and had "projected" those trends into the early 1970s; when this growth failed to materialise they cut back on their earlier massive orders, and manufacturers saw their production rates fluctuate wildly from year to year. In 1972–73, Boeing made determined efforts to reduce their dependence on the air-

liner industry, taking part in a number of contests to meet military requirements, but they were not generally successful: Lockheed frustrated their efforts to fill a niche in the anti-submarine warfare market, while the potentially very large USAF Medium Short Take-Off/Landing (STOL) Transport programme did not proceed into production.

Following their recovery in the early 1970s, however, Boeing set out on a career of increasing prosperity. Revamped in "Advanced" versions, the 727 and 737 were the foundation of the company's fortunes. The 727 proved that it could still compete in passenger appeal with the big trijets, and on the US domestic market the recession delayed introduction of the wide-bodies and gave the 727 a new lease of life. Meanwhile, the 737 made up a lot of competitive ground on the DC-9, hitherto the market leader among twinjets.

The fourth wide-body producer, the European Airbus Industrie consortium, ran two years behind their rivals, and this was nearly their undoing. Air transport had just begun to emerge from the recession of the early 1970s when, in October 1973, war flared up again in the Middle East. Following the use of the oil embargo by the Arab states, the Organisation of Petroleum Exporting Countries (OPEC) decided on a massive rise in fuel prices. Had the Airbus consortium not been backed by the French and German Governments, and had it not been for the fact that the project was an expression of the Europeans' political will to compete in the aerospace market, the fuel crisis would probably have spelt its end. As it was, the rise in costs and the consequent drastic recession in air transport (harder hit than almost any other industry)

killed off a BAC-led venture to build
Europlane, a smaller rival to the
A300. By the time the A300 entered
service in 1974, Air France were the
only major, firm customer. The
German flag carrier, Lufthansa were
theoretically on the books, but traffic
on their domestic and European
routes appeared to be declining in
the face of rising costs, and Lufthansa
did not think the European routes
were ready to accept the A300; they
were prepared to fight any decision
forcing them to accept an aircraft
which they did not want, and
Lufthansa orders remained options
for a considerable time.

Throughout 1974, the A300 remained a poor seller, despite the fact
that technically it was proving a
great success. It had been stretched
somewhat during its development,
and the production aircraft were
slightly longer than the A300B1
prototypes. The initial service version was the A300B2, weighing
302,000 lb at take-off, but in 1975
Airbus flew the first A300B4, with
347,000 lb gross weight, more fuel

and a greater range. Later development took both types to higher
weights; from 1979, Airbus could
deliver the 363,000 lb A300B4-200,
which could carry a full, 280-
passenger, mixed-class load over a
2,500-mile sector.

In numbers of passenger seats, the
A300 was only fractionally smaller
than the US trijets, but the crucial
difference was that the A300 was
optimised for shorter ranges than the
TriStar or DC-10. The designers of
the European twin also avoided the
awkward, trijet layout; compared
with the simple twin, the trijet needs
a larger tailfin and tailplane (because
the rear fuselage is shorter, due to the
weight of the rear engine), while the
rear engine installation is complex
and needs a lot of fuel and control
runs. A twin-engined aircraft is also
more reliable (because there are
fewer engines to make trouble),
although airworthiness rules limit
the distance it can fly over water or
away from a diversion airfield. Later
versions of the A300 were to achieve
payload-range performance not

In 1977, Airbus Industrie delivered aircraft to Thai International and Aerocondor. Two other aircraft are seen before painting

much inferior to that of the TriStar or DC-10-10, with two engines instead of three. (The A300 power-plants were, of course, uprated CF6-50s developed for the intercontinental DC-10-30, rather than the lower-powered units fitted to the DC-10-10.) Part of the credit for this went to the small, highly loaded wing, and its very efficient system of double-slotted flaps and leading-edge slats.

However, by the time the A300 appeared, many of the world's biggest airlines had already ordered TriStars or DC-10-10s, and many of them thought that the A300 was too close in size to the trijets to operate on the same fleet. Although Airbus signed up a number of customers in 1975, the following year produced virtually no orders in the face of a withering counter-attack by Boeing. The Germans in particular had strong doubts as to whether it was worth carrying on with the programme; few observers noticed, however, that the short-range US versions of the DC-10 and TriStar had

not attracted a single new customer since the A300 had appeared on the scene.

Meanwhile, after the rise in fuel prices, McDonnell Douglas and Lockheed found that the market was simply not large enough to support economical production of their almost identical domestic trijets. With the recession in traffic growth, Lockheed found that their TriStar salesmen were competing directly with men from Eastern Airlines, who were trying to sell their airline's own TriStars straight off the production line. DC-10 and TriStar production rates were low, so unit costs were high; prices were pared to the bone, and both manufacturers lost money.

Lockheed were also in trouble when Japan's All Nippon Airways ordered the TriStar after a close-fought contest with the DC-10-10 in 1972. Lockheed, still seeking US Government backing for their financial overdraft, had to open their books to US Government officials. Substantial discrepancies and unauthorised payments were found, it

being discovered in due course that
massive bribes had been paid to
secure the All Nippon order. Although, in many parts of the world,
bribery is the rule rather than the
exception when large orders for commercial aircraft are in prospect, the
US public investigation of the Lockheed scandal did not help the
company's sales campaign.

Indirectly, the ANA order sparked
off a chain of events which was
to lead to problems for McDonnell
Douglas. ANA's decision to buy the
TriStar had been sudden; so sudden,
in fact, that McDonnell Douglas
already had six DC-10s destined for
ANA on the production line. They
had been ordered by the Japanese
trading company Mitsui, which
hoped to resell them to ANA. With
ANA's TriStar order, these aircraft
became surplus. At that time, they
missed a modification which was
applied to the rear cargo door on all
DC-10s following a near-disaster to
an American Airlines aircraft. The
unmodified aircraft were resold to
Laker Airways and to Turkish Airlines (THY). In March 1974, one of
the THY aircraft lost its cargo door
while climbing out of Paris Orly
airport. The depressurisation rup-

tured the floor, tearing the control
lines and jamming the elevators in
the up position and the DC-10
crashed with the loss of 347 lives.

The investigation of the DC-10
crash – the first total-fatality loss of a
wide-body aircraft – cast a shadow
on McDonnell Douglas' reputation
for sound engineering, but hardly
offset the market lead which they
had established over Lockheed by
the early development of the long-
range DC-10-30/40, for which Lockheed had no rival. Sales of the DC-10-
30 allowed McDonnell Douglas to
hold higher production rates than
Lockheed while the medium-range
business was in the doldrums; Lockheed found that they could not afford
to produce an equivalent version of
the TriStar, because there was no
launch customer big enough to
justify it and there was no version of
the RB.211 equivalent to the CF6-50.

By 1973, the DC-10-30 was causing
problems for the 747 as well as for
the TriStar. Boeing were finding that
airlines had burned their fingers by
ordering large batches of 747s before
traffic growth had slowed down, and
that they were now buying long-
range DC-10s instead. The DC-10,
with three engines instead of four,

was cheaper to run than the 747, although this advantage was more than offset by the greater capacity of the Boeing. But the airlines preferred to play safe and buy the smaller aircraft. The last straw for Boeing came when Pan American decided that they needed a smaller aircraft than the standard 747. In order to keep the DC-10-30/40 out of the fleet of their biggest customer, Boeing decided to build a modified 747 which, instead of being stretched in the traditional way, would be no less than 47 ft *shorter* than standard.

The result, the 747SP (Special Performance), was the most controversial of all the wide-body aircraft. Because of its low wing loading and high power-to-weight ratio, it could fly high, and it could fly further than any other airliner. It was also capable of operating out of hot-and-high airfields where other airliners were severely limited in their payload and range. The wing and engines of the SP were the same as those of the standard 747 (although the complex trailing-edge flaps of the standard aircraft were replaced by a much simpler system) and the aircraft was very costly to operate; some 747 operators found that a few SPs could be added to an existing fleet to tackle special routes; Pan Am, for instance, used their first SPs to start a non-stop New York – Tokyo service. Smaller operators with hot-and-high problems or a need for extreme range, such as South African Airways or Iran Air, also bought SPs. However, most airlines were totally uninterested in the 747SP, which they regarded as hopelessly uneconomical. It is unlikely that Boeing will ever sell enough SPs to recover the development costs directly, but the company may consider that the protection of the 747 market against the DC-10 was worth the trouble.

By 1974, it could clearly be seen that Boeing's next new aircraft would be a replacement for the 727. This would not only be enormously expensive to develop, but the eventual decline of the 727 would leave the 747 as the company's main breadwinner, supporting development of the new type. While Boeing studied what shape the new aircraft should take, the company applied their renowned expertise in product development to the 747. Freighter and convertible versions were already in service by 1974, but in that year, the Belgian flag carrier Sabena asked for a new version in which only the rear half of the cabin would be convertible. Rather to Boeing's surprise, this so-called Combi version proved highly popular; cheaper and lighter than a full convertible (because the heavy freight floor did not have to be so big) it gave operators the chance to alter the mix of passenger-to-freight traffic from season to season.

Boeing also continued to offer higher weights on the 747: in 1975, the company delivered a heavier version of the 747B, grossing up to 805,000 lb and carrying extra fuel in the outer wings. The "820K" airframe (at 820,000 lb) followed soon after.

The Seattle company actively encouraged all the engine manufacturers to get their engines aboard the 747, knowing the competition among the engine makers would be good for the customer and for Boeing. Both General Electric and Rolls-Royce eventually sold engines for the 747, and in 1978 it was still the only aircraft to have flown with all three big-fan engines. GE's success spurred Pratt & Whitney to develop a new version of the JT9D, the 7Q, specifically for the 747. The total effect of airframe and engine improvements over the life of the 747 was so great that some airlines (including Lufthansa and Singapore Airlines) decided to sell their entire 747 fleets and replace them with the much improved later models. By late 1978, the 747 line was running at its highest feasible pace, and, despite the fact that Boeing were asking nearly $20 million more for a 747 than Douglas were for the DC-10-30, the production line was booked out to mid-1981. The pre-set break-even point of 400 sales was passed in mid-1978, although the development of the SP and other derivatives had probably pushed the actual break-even figure well beyond this.

The decision to fit the Rolls-Royce RB.211 to the 747 was made

in mid-1975, but the development of the necessarily more powerful version of this engine had been started before that time for the Lockheed TriStar and its derivatives. The uprated, RB.211-524, offering up to 50,000 lb-thrust, removed the main block to Lockheed's development of a TriStar rival to the long-haul DC-10s. Lockheed were quick to offer the TriStar 200, basically similar to the standard aircraft but rather heavier, weighing 466,000 lb for take-off. This was considerably less than the DC-10-30 and the TriStar 200 lacked the extended wing tips and centre landing gear of the McDonnell Douglas type, so it was not a direct competitor. However, a British Airways requirement in late 1975 for a VC10 competitor gave Lockheed their opportunity to enter the long-haul game in earnest. Lock-

heed's proposal to British Airways was the TriStar 500, 20 ft shorter than the standard aircraft. During the course of the sales battle which followed, with McDonnell Douglas offering a Rolls-Royce-powered version of the DC-10-30 in competition, the TriStar 500 grew 6 ft 6 in back towards the original TriStar 100. Passenger capacity was still smaller than that of the DC-10, and the cost per seat-mile was slightly higher, but the Lockheed team hoped that the lower aircraft-mile cost of the TriStar 500 would carry the day. After a hard-fought contest, British Airways ordered the 500; the new version flew in October 1978 and went into service in early 1979. Compared with the DC-10-30, the TriStar 500 was smaller and cheaper to operate. It was thus a formidable competitor when airlines came to consider a

One of the modified versions of established types to appear during the second half of the 1970s was Lockheed's TriStar 500. Later versions will have "active ailerons"

Boeing 747B of China Airlines

replacement for their 707s and DC-8s. In April 1978, the TriStar 500 won an order from Pan Am; Boeing were less than pleased, because the Seattle company had spent a great deal of money on the 747SP just to stop Pan Am buying the DC-10. Finally, it was Lockheed who reaped the benefit.

Always adventurous in new technology, Lockheed applied a number of new systems to the TriStar 500. It was the first airliner designed to make use of "active controls." The ailerons were designed to be linked to an automatic control system which sensed vertical accelerations and deflected the ailerons simultaneously to counter the movement. The ailerons thus opposed the bending forces on the wing, and Lockheed were able to produce a longer-span wing, reducing drag, for the same structural weight. The TriStar 500 also introduced an advanced avionic system intended to manage the controls, helping the crew adhere to best cruise speeds and reducing fuel burn.

The Soviet Union did not want to be left behind in the wide-body race. The Ilyushin bureau was asked in the early 1970s to design a wide-body for Aeroflot, and impressions of the first design appeared in 1971. The Il-86, in its initial form, was a straightforward adaptation of the long-haul Ilyushin Il-62, with the same wing, tail unit and Soloviev D-30KP powerplants married to a twin-aisle fuselage seating 250 pas-

A spectacular study of a Royal Air
Maroc 747B Combi. The mixed-
traffic Combi is the most popular
747 variant among small airlines

sengers. The type was intended for
use on Aeroflot's high-density internal routes, such as the holiday
flights from Moscow to the Black Sea
resorts. The use of the low-bypass-
ratio Soloviev turbofan showed the
West that the Soviet aircraft industry
had not yet produced a successful
big-fan engine. The lack of a suitable
powerplant continued to hinder
Soviet plans for a wide-body airliner,
and the USSR became concerned at
the effects on national prestige should
Western airliners start operating
their advanced equipment into
Russia and her satellite countries. In
1973–75, the Soviet Union took the
unprecedented step of negotiating
with Western firms for the construction of a massive new airliner factory,

in which a Western design would be
produced under licence. Lockheed
came closest to filling this requirement, but the move was blocked
because of the dangers of technology
transfer and the Russians were forced
to fall back on the Il-86, which
underwent a major redesign following its debut in model form. By 1973,
the configuration had changed completely, to become the first Soviet
airliner to make use of podded
engines. (Soviet military aircraft
using this layout had included Professor Baade's EF 150, and Ilyushin's
own Il-54 Blowlamp, a supersonic
development of the Baade design.)
Later, it was decided to use more
powerful Kuznetsov NK-86 engines
in place of the Soloviev units, and

the gross weight of the aircraft was increased to 420,000 lb. Like the Tu-154, the Il-86 had a full complement of high-lift devices, including triple-slotted trailing-edge flaps and full-span leading-edge slats. The NK-86, however, was still a low-bypass-ratio engine, and this penalised the performance of the Il-86. Its payload-range performance was only slightly better than that of the A300B4-200 which was some 60,000 lb lighter. A unique feature of the Il-86 was its use of the lower deck as a passenger-boarding area; passengers entered the aircraft via built-in airstairs on the lower deck, and deposited their baggage in racks before walking upstairs into the passenger cabin.

The Il-86 flew in late 1976 and entered service in 1979 on Aeroflot's high-density domestic and European routes. It was also ordered by LOT,

the Polish airline, and a large proportion of the airframe work was carried out by WSK-Mielec in Poland. The Soviet Union wanted to conserve its own efforts for a proposed long-haul derivative of the Il-86, but development was delayed by the lack of a Russian high-bypass-ratio engine of the necessary power; the West was still blocking the export of such high-technology engines to a potential enemy. The Soviet Union made several attempts to buy small batches of Western engines, ostensibly for flight-test purposes, but Western governments and manufacturers feared that the Soviet Union would simply strip the engines and analyse them minutely in order to copy the techniques used in their manufacture.

By the time the Il-86 made its debut, Western manufacturers were proceeding with the definition of

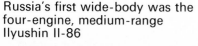
Russia's first wide-body was the four-engine, medium-range Ilyushin Il-86

another new generation of aircraft. Just as the technology of the 707 and DC-8 had been scaled down for the world's shorter routes, producing the 727 and the twinjets, so the technology of the wide-bodies was to be applied to smaller aircraft. Fuel costs were clearly going to be the main driving force: the savings from more efficient engines and airframes would be substantial. Traffic growth was also a factor: the industry assumed, rightly, that the fuel crisis only meant a pause in the expansion of traffic, and that bigger aircraft would be needed to replace the world's 727s. However, the immediate problem of traffic congestion, which had been on everyone's mind when the first wide-bodies were designed, seemed less urgent.

Noise, however, was still a problem. The manufacturers had done well in making the 747, DC-10 and TriStar no noisier, and in many cases

far quieter, than the much lighter 707s and DC-8s, but this had only arrested the growth of the noise problem. The next aim was to achieve an actual reduction in noise nuisance despite continuing traffic growth. In the late 1960s, US and international authorities adopted new noise rules with which all aircraft would eventually have to comply. The US Federal Aviation Administration rules were set out in Part 36 of the Federal Aviation Regulations (FAR 36), while the International Civil Aviation Organisation (ICAO) regulations, which were closely similar in their effect, were laid down by Annex 16 of the Convention which originally established ICAO. Annex 16 standards were adopted by many countries, while some used the US rules.

FAR 36 and Annex 16 originally set noise standards for new types of aircraft, but they were gradually

Air transport in the 1970s: DC-10 and 747s at Amsterdam Schiphol Airport extended to cover more and more aircraft in service. Effectively, they set an upper noise limit for an aircraft of given weight at three fixed monitoring points: one just beneath the final approach, one beneath the climb-out path and one to the side of the runway. The 707 and DC-8 would need extensive modifications to comply with the new rules; the 727 and the twinjets would meet them with relatively minor changes, while most of the wide-bodies were well within the limits (the only exceptions being some early 747s). From the early 1970s, US airlines were no longer allowed to buy new 707s, while all new 737s, DC-9s and 727s had to be equipped with sound-absorbent materials in the nacelles to meet the new rules. In 1977, the US Government decreed that all aircraft not meeting FAR 36 by the end of 1985 would have to be retired, and similar actions were taken in several other countries.

The mid-1970s, however, saw the formulation of an even tougher set of rules aimed at the new generation of smaller aircraft then being proposed. New US rules were drafted under FAR 36, while the ICAO rules were known as CAN 5 after the organisation's Fifth Committee on Aircraft Noise, which had prepared them. The new rules presupposed the application of big-fan technology to the new, smaller aircraft.

Although the new aircraft would be far less of a technical advance than the wide-bodies had been, manufacturers nevertheless hoped for considerable benefits from new aerofoil technology. Great strides had been made in this area in the late 1960s and early 1970s, particularly with the application of computer technology to what had always been a slightly philosophical area of aircraft design. The wing of the 747, for instance, was designed with a better understanding of the behaviour of air at near-sonic speeds than that of the 707 had been, and the 747 was thus able to cruise faster and more efficiently than its ancestor. The A300, arriving on the scene rather later, drew on British research into advanced aerofoils to produce a wing that was thicker and lighter than

earlier designs, but could cruise at the same speed.

Research by the US National Aeronautics and Space Administration (NASA) in the early 1970s produced a great deal of information about such advanced aerofoils. The distinguishing feature of such advanced sections was the fact that much of the airflow above the wing was moving faster than sound; hence the term "supercritical" coined by NASA to describe their own designs. Before the fuel crisis, it was thought that the new technology would be used to produce an airliner cruising just above the speed of sound, faster than ordinary aircraft but not fast enough to leave a sonic boom on the ground. After the fuel crisis, it was clear that the new technology would be better employed in saving drag and weight, and hence fuel.

Engine technology appeared to reach a plateau in the mid-1970s. The main reason was that the low fuel consumption of the big-fan engines had been partly offset by their very high maintenance costs and – in some cases – mediocre reliability. Although the engine manufacturers all worked hard on "maturity programmes" aimed at getting their engines to settle down in service, it was clear that the high costs were an inevitable result of the search for high pressure ratios and for high performance from every part of the engine. The behaviour of the big-fan engines came as something of a shock to the airlines, and they were totally unreceptive to the idea of another generation. Two smaller engines were, however, launched in the first half of the 1970s. The first was the Franco-American CFM56, developed by the French Snecma company in co-operation with GE in a bid to break Rolls-Royce's monopoly of engine manufacture in Europe; the second was Pratt & Whitney's JT10D.

Another promising area of new technology was the development of "composite" materials for aircraft structures, such as the carbon fibres which had got Rolls-Royce into trouble on the RB.211. The manufacturers proceeded with considerable caution, as the characteristics of the new materials were almost completely different from the qualities of aluminium, and it was hard to predict how well composites would stand up to a long service life in unfavourable climatic conditions. However, composites offered substantial weight savings in certain areas; one of the first applications was on Concorde, which used carbonfibre brake pads rather than conventional steel brakes.

In avionics, digital technology was promising to replace older, analogue systems. The digital systems substituted electronics for moving parts; they were thus more reliable, more compact and more capable than the traditional autopilots and navigation systems. They could also drive new, versatile displays, including head-up displays which allowed the pilot to follow his instruments while looking out of the cockpit. By presenting information to the crew in more easily digestible forms, they could help the crew fly more efficiently and more safely. On the advanced flight decks of new-generation aircraft, large TV-type displays are likely to replace many of the old-fashioned banks of dials and warning lights.

Apart from the supercritical wing, however, most of these improvements could be applied to existing aircraft, and one of the main arguments, as the airlines and manufacturers sought to define the new generation, was over the merits of expensive, all-new aircraft as opposed to cheaper derivatives of existing types.

The other great debate was over which manufacturers would design and build the new aircraft. The 727-replacement market called for, at most, two types of aircraft, and the lesson of the TriStar versus DC-10 contest was clear: for two manufacturers to engage in head-on competition in the same market slot would probably prevent either from making a profit. It seemed likely that at least one of the major concerns in the business would opt out of the short/medium-haul market. If the Europeans insisted on their own programmes in both market sectors, times might be hard for the Americans. Boeing, with 60 per cent

Space is at a premium in the crowded final-assembly hangar for the A300 and A310. A production rate of eight aircraft a month is achievable

of the existing market, were determined to retain their dominant position. Their first aim was to convince United Airlines, the western world's biggest carrier and the biggest potential customer for a 727-replacement. Boeing's discussions with United were to last more than four years. In late 1973, Boeing offered a stretched 727 to United. Discussions continued for more than 18 months, and by mid-1975 Boeing were well advanced with the design of the 727-300B, as the new aircraft was to be called. Compared with the 727-200, it was 20 ft longer and used the new JT8D-217 engine, fitted with a larger fan for more power and less noise. A new bogie landing gear was fitted, and the aircraft would have been fitted with similar leading-edge devices to those of the 747. The 727 prototype was flown with the new high-lift system and Boeing confidently expected to launch the programme in the autumn of 1975; in August of that year it came as a severe shock to the company when United said they did not want the aircraft.

By that time, however, Boeing were already looking hard at an all-new aircraft, under the designation 7X7. Originally proposed with a "semi-wide-body" fuselage, seating seven passengers abreast, and with three CFM56s or JT10Ds, the 7X7 evolved into an eight-abreast twin looking very like an A300, but rather shorter. It would seat around 200 passengers.

Airbus Industrie were looking at a similarly sized aircraft, derived from

Among the configurations studied by Boeing for their 7X7 was this T-tailed trijet

the A300 with a shortened fuselage and designated A300B10, but realised that they first had to get the basic A300 moving on the sales front. If Airbus tried to launch the B10, it would be taken as confirmation of the sales line which Boeing had been using for some time – that the A300 was simply too big for the market. Boeing encouraged Airbus to discuss possible collaboration on the A300B10 or the 7X7 for this very reason, and it was not until September 1976 that the European consortium firmly decided not to build the B10 until the A300 could stand up for itself.

McDonnell Douglas had looked at the possibility of building a twin-engined version of the DC-10 in direct competition with the A300 as early as 1973, and in 1975 proposed a smaller aircraft, still based on the DC-10 fuselage section. Designated DC-X-200, it would have had a new,

supercritical wing. Lockheed also studied short-fuselage and twin-engined versions of the TriStar.

All three US manufacturers were actively seeking partners overseas to help them develop their new projects; they had various reasons for doing this, perhaps the most important being the sheer size of the investment necessary to develop and put into production any new airliner. If a large section of the project could be hived-off to a risk-sharing partner, failure of the programme would not necessarily put the whole company at risk. For the US manufacturers, collaboration with Europe meant that Airbus Industrie would not be competing directly with their own products; alternatively, a collaborative deal with the soon-to-be-nationalised British aerospace industry would keep the British out of Airbus Industrie and forestall a dangerous strengthening of that con-

sortium. Co-operation with Europe would also offer access to European markets. While exploring major partnerships with Britain or Germany, Boeing were also working on smaller deals to off-load a considerable proportion of their development work on the 7X7. Discussions with Italy and Japan continued as definition of the aircraft proceeded.

Following the demise of the 727-300B, Boeing also began to study a family of more advanced aircraft based on their current, narrow-body designs. The new, 7N7 family tended to grow during development, and by September 1976 Boeing were proposing the 7N7-143, as big as the 727-300B and powered by two, new "cropped-fan" engines. These were to be based on the same core as the existing big-fan engines, but would be fitted with smaller fans and run at lower temperatures. Although they would not be quite as efficient as the

full-sized engines, they would be far cheaper to develop than a new engine aimed at the same thrust bracket and, with lower operating temperatures and pressures, should be easier to maintain.

By mid-1977, Boeing were in a quandary: the biggest 7N7 seemed to rival the 7X7, which at that time was proposed with three, cropped-fan engines. The two types could be seen as complementary, because they differed considerably in range although they were fairly close in seating capacity, but if they were developed in parallel this would mean an enormous development bill for the company. United seemed keen on the low costs of the 7N7, while American Airlines, another important customer, wanted the longer range and twin-aisle comfort of the 7X7.

As Boeing continued to waver, Airbus Industrie recovered from

The 1978 "war of the paper aeroplanes" culminated in a United Airlines order for the 200-seat, twin-engined Boeing 767-200

225

above
Airbus Industrie's biggest breakthrough came in 1978, with the sale of 23 aircraft to Eastern Airlines in the USA

opposite, top
Among the new types launched in 1978 was the narrow-bodied Boeing 757, designed as a successor to the 727. The T-tail configuration was later dropped in favour of a more conventional design

opposite, bottom
Airbus Industrie's short-body A310 will be Europe's counter to the Boeing 767, seating about 210 passengers and due for certification in 1982

their run of misfortune. In April 1977, Eastern Airlines agreed to take four A300s on loan for a six-month operational trial – Europe's first breakthrough in the US market since the One-Eleven 400 was sold to American and Mohawk. Airbus then proceeded to score a number of important successes among European flag airlines and in the Far East. In April 1978, Eastern placed firm orders for the A300, and by that time Airbus Industrie's existing customers had projected future needs for more than 300 of the big twins. In early 1978, the French and German Governments confirmed their intention of building the smaller A300B10 and getting it into service by 1983 at latest. Before then, in late 1977, United Airlines announced that they, too, were studying the A300B10.

Boeing were now getting worried: an attempt to produce a compromise

between 7N7 and 7X7 for United and American, with a seven-abreast fuselage and cropped-fan engines, seemed to have been unsuccessful. However, another proposal with the same section, but with full-size engines, had more appeal for United. American wanted an aircraft about the same size, but with a longer range and three smaller engines. Boeing realised that they might have to do both, and in February 1978, allotted the designation 767 to the twin, and 777 to the trijet.

By 1978, Boeing were faced with another challenge in the middle of their product range, from the McDonnell Douglas DC-9 Super 80, which used the new, refanned Pratt & Whitney JT8D-209 and did for the DC-9 what the -300B would have done for Boeing's 727. The appeal of the Super 80 was that its development costs were low and that it was cheap to operate, especially on short

routes. With its appearance, the DC-9 was confirmed as the most stretched aircraft in history – the Super 80's passenger cabin was nearly twice as long as that of the original DC-9-10, and could accommodate more than 170 passengers in a high-density layout. The Super 80 was launched with an order from Swissair in October 1977, and the prototype flew in mid-1979. As well as the new engines and an enlarged wing, the Super 80 introduced a new digital autopilot.

A number of manufacturers had proposed aircraft to fill this market slot, but by the beginning of 1978 McDonnell Douglas were the only ones to have gone ahead. BAC (now part of British Aerospace) had proposed developed versions of the One-Eleven, first with refanned engines and later with CFM56s. By 1977, the company were looking at the X-Eleven, using the One-Eleven

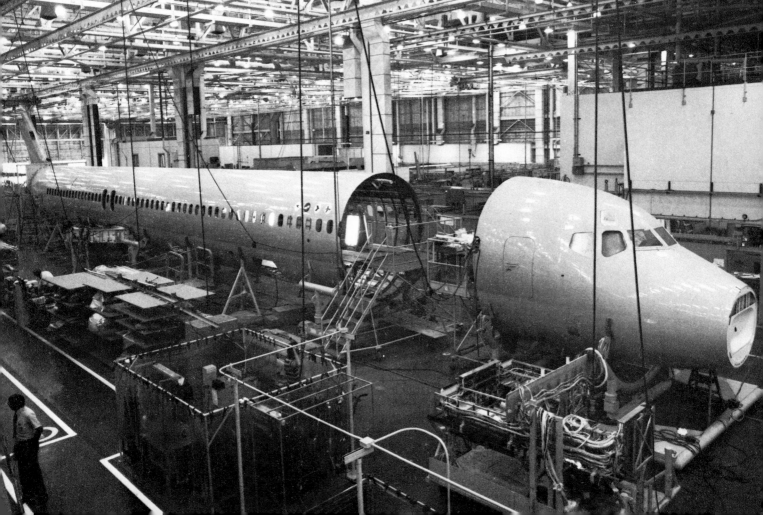

wing and tail married to a new fuselage seating six passengers abreast. France came quite close to fitting CFM56s to a stretched version of the Mercure, but in late 1977 the two countries shelved their national projects in favour of a new, twin-CFM56 aircraft called the Joint European Transport (Jet).

Boeing made the next positive move: at the same time as they allotted the designations 767 and 777 to their twin-aisle twin and trijet aircraft, they applied the designation 757 to a narrow-body twin aimed at British Airways and Eastern Airlines. By the time the two airlines ordered the type, it had grown until it was larger than the 7N7-143 of September 1976 and nearly as big as the 767, with two Rolls-Royce RB.211-535 cropped-fan engines. The first 757 is due to fly in 1982.

In July 1978, Lufthansa and Swissair confirmed their interest in the 200-seat A300B10 – redesignated A310 – and within a matter of weeks United Airlines announced an order for the 767. Both these big twins are now due to fly in 1981, and should enter service in the second half of 1982. The decisions of 1978 set the scene for the sales battles of the 1980s. The first rounds went to Boeing with Delta and American ordering a heavier version of the 767 with non-stop transcontinental range. Throughout the spring and summer of 1978, Boeing and Rolls-Royce mounted a campaign to persuade British Aerospace to join the 757 programme rather than Airbus Industrie, but in October of that year, British Aerospace agreed to take a share in the European consortium. Boeing, who had already agreed to share 767 development with the Japanese and Italians, then had to seek a manufacturing partner in the USA to share the risks of the 757.

Still on the drawing boards in late 1978 were projects such as the European Jet, McDonnell Douglas' ATMR (about the same size as the Boeing 757) and Fokker-VFW's F.29, powered by Rolls-Royce RB.432s. However, much of the market seemed likely to be dominated by existing types for many years.

Of the aircraft still in production, the oldest were the Boeing 707 and Fokker-VFW's F.27. The latter, along with the similar but slightly later British Aerospace 748, was still selling slowly to military and civil customers, and both companies were developing maritime-patrol versions of their aircraft. Neither of these twin-Dart types appeared to have been seriously hurt by the arrival of the de Havilland Canada Dash 7. Similar in size and range to the established F.27 and 748, but powered by four small Pratt & Whitney PT6A-50 turboprops, the Dash 7 was specially designed for

opposite, top
Hawaiian Air were among the customers for Douglas' massively stretched DC-9 Super 80

opposite, bottom
McDonnell Douglas launched their 172-seat DC-9 Super 80 in 1977

top
The European Jet project aims to offer substantial improvements in noise and fuel consumption

above
Crowded Boeing 727 and 737 production lines shared the same Renton hangar in 1978

229

operations from short runways, particularly near city centres. However, few operators could afford its relatively high price and maintenance costs, and sales appear to have been limited to airlines with specialised requirements. Flown in 1975, the Dash 7 entered service with Rocky Mountain Airways in late 1977.

Sales of the 707 for airline operations had virtually stopped by 1978, but the line was kept open by government customers and the US Air Force, who had chosen the 707 as the basis for their E-3A Sentry Airborne Warning And Control System (AWACS) aircraft. Britain was then producing its own AWACS aircraft from the Nimrod development of the de Havilland Comet.) The 707, however, received a new lease of life in early 1977, when it was decided to fit a 707 with four advanced CFM56 turbofans. A production 707-700 – as the aircraft would be designated – would not only comfortably meet the new CAN

5 noise rules, but could be stretched to carry 180 passengers over the same range as the standard 707-320C.

The 727 was still going strong at the end of 1978, with continuing re-orders even from the biggest US airlines. Although it was being replaced in Boeing's planning by the 757, it had already passed the 1,500-sales mark in early 1978. The third of the Boeing narrow-bodies, the 737, seemed set to go on until the mid-1980s at least, with a continuing programme of improvements to keep it attractive. In 1978, the 737 won a major order from British Airways, an unusual achievement for an aircraft which had been in production for 12 years.

Of the other twinjets, the DC-9 was progressing towards 1,000 sales with the aid of the new Super 80. Production of the F.28 and One-Eleven was proceeding more slowly; the latter may well be built in Romania from the mid-1980s, becoming the first Western airliner to

be licence-built in an East European country.

New types in the short-haul market include the British Aerospace 146: this was launched by Hawker Siddeley in 1973, before the nationalisation of the British industry, but was cancelled the following year because of the recession caused by the fuel price rises. In 1978, however, the project was relaunched by British Aerospace, and the first 146s are now due to enter service in late 1981. The 146 is unusual in having four engines – US-built Avco Lycoming ALF 502s – and a high wing. The four-engine layout was chosen because only the ALF 502 appeared to offer the combination of low noise and low costs that the designers were looking for. The engine uses the core section of the military T55 turbine, geared to a new fan. The wing of the 146 will also be built in the USA by Avco.

Another new short-hauler is the Soviet Yakovlev Yak-42, a 120-

above
Boeing have been strong in the Middle East and North Africa since the beginning of the jet age. This 707-320C for Libyan Arab Airlines was one of the last of the type to be delivered to an airline customer

opposite, top
The de Havilland Canada Dash 7 made its maiden flight in March 1975

opposite, bottom
Aeroflot's 120-seater Yakovlev Yak-42 trijet makes its Western debut at the Paris air show, 1977

231

above
The Yakolev Yak-40 features a broad, unswept wing with simple flaps. There are plans to build a derivative in the USA

right
Originally conceived as a swing-nose passenger/freight convertible aircraft, the VFW 614 became a 44-seat short-haul jet with its podded engines mounted above the wing. The type was basically too expensive for the market, however, and production ceased in 1977

seater with three high-bypass-ratio Lotarev D-36 turbofans. The Soviet team took the unusual step of building two prototypes with different wings for comparative evaluation before selecting a 25° wing in favour of a less sharply swept design. The Yak-42 has a very large, simple wing (there are no leading-edge devices) and a very high power-to-weight ratio. It will replace Il-18s and Tu-134s on shorter Aeroflot routes, and was due to enter service in 1979. The D-36, Russia's first high-bypass-ratio powerplant, is a three-shaft engine not unlike a scaled-down RB.211, and is thus more complex than later Western designs (such as the RB.432) of comparable size.

Even smaller airliners include the 32-seat Yakolev Yak-40, predecessor of the Yak-42. Between 1970 and 1976, considerable efforts were made to gain certification for the Yak-40, which with its unswept wing and three simple turbofans seemed to

offer attractive economics, but the technical difficulties in the path of certifying such an aircraft in the West proved severe, and Aviaexport, the Soviet agency in charge of selling airliners outside the Soviet bloc, eventually gave up their attempts to sell the Yak-40 and transferred their efforts to the Yak-42.

West Germany's airliner programme started in the early 1960s. The Weser 614 was to be a convertible aircraft with a swing nose for loading freight and with two Lycoming turbofans mounted on pylons above the unswept wing. By the time it flew in 1972, it had become the VFW 614, and its manufacturer was part of the multinational VFW-Fokker combine. The swing nose had been abandoned, and the aircraft was now a 44-seater with M45H engines. This engine type was the only survivor of a range of powerplants developed jointly by Bristol Siddeley and Snecma in the 1960s;

The Canadair Challenger business jet may form the basis of a future commuter airliner

above
German feeder-line General Air were one of the first Western airlines to introduce a Soviet-built aircraft, the Yak-40. The experiment was not successful

right
With its quiet, five-blade propellers, the Shorts 330 carries up to 30 passengers on short sectors

a related engine, the M45G, was to have powered an Anglo-French supersonic strike fighter. The M45H was a costly engine to buy and to maintain, and the 614 itself was basically too expensive for the market. Production ceased in late 1977 after a handful had been sold. Canadair's Challenger executive jet may be developed into an airliner in the same basic category, if market demand is adequate.

Less ambitious but more successful than the 614 is the Shorts 330, built in Northern Ireland. It closely resembles that company's earlier Skyvan, with a box-like fuselage, a very-high-aspect-ratio wing and twin tailfins. Interestingly, it has a few more seats (30) than a DC-3 and

234

about as much power, with two Canadian-built PT6A turboprops (as used on the Dash 7). Although the 330 is slow and unpressurised, this does not make much difference on the short flights such aircraft usually make, and the Shorts aircraft has a more roomy cabin and carries more payload than most of its competitors.

These aircraft are likely to carry the bulk of the world's air traffic through the 1980s and 1990s. Whatever new technologies may be introduced, the current new types will retain their advantage over the next decade at least; by 1990, the oldest 747 will be 20 years old, with 90,000 hours or more on its airframes. At that time the airline world may start to look for new technology.

Airliners of the future

Throughout the first half of the 1980s, the airliner manufacturers will be preoccupied with development of the new aircraft types launched in the late 1970s in both the USA and Europe. The subsonic airliner has been developed to a high pitch of efficiency with the advent of the wide-body airliners, and these types may be in production well into the next century. Historically, passenger aircraft have tended to remain in production for longer and longer as the industry has expanded. The biplane airliners of the 1920s were superseded by bigger and more powerful aircraft almost every year. The Boeing 247 reigned only briefly as queen of the skies before it was overtaken by the DC-2. Even the classic DC-3 lasted a mere five years in first-line service before faster Lockheeds and high-flying Boeing 307s threatened its dominance of the major US trunk routes (it was military production which made the DC3 a classic).

A break in this pattern came in the post-war era, when the Douglas DC-4, the Lockheed Constellation and their descendants dominated the air routes for some 13 years, despite the fact that both had been designed before the war, some six years before they entered airline service. On the other hand, the last DC-7Cs and Starliners were very different aircraft from their transcontinental-range forbears. It could be said that new technology, such as improved aerodynamics and structures (as in the Starliner wing, the DC-6 pressurisation system and the Wright turbo-compound engine) had been incorporated in the basic designs. Another factor was the Korean War and the "Cold War", and the consequent massive re-equipment of Western air forces with jets, which dominated the manufacturing in-dustry and contributed to the long life of the piston giants.

It was the pressure of commercial competition, and the determination of such manufacturers as de Havilland and Boeing to break the Lockheed/Douglas hold on the market, which brought in the jets in 1958. Not until the first fully developed jets appeared (the Boeing 707-320C and the Douglas DC-8-50) did their economics prove superior to those of the piston airliner. The first jets, however, created the travel boom that led to their replacement as well as establishing the technology which made it possible. The introduction of wide-body jets was motivated by the increasing problems of noise and congestion, as well as the availability of wing and engine technology which would make the aircraft cheaper to operate.

Do the conditions for the launch of a new generation of airliners, replacements for the 747 and other wide-bodies, exist in the industry? Will these conditions emerge in the 1980s? It is almost certain that the main factor in determining the need for a new generation will be the price of fuel. The airlines became used to cheap fuel in the 1950s and 1960s, when the expansion of air travel made the supply of aviation fuel far more economical. (Much of the price of aviation fuel is accounted for by the cost of getting that fuel to the airports, the price of crude and its refining processes being only part of the total.) Just after the oil-price increases of 1973–74, fuel had done no more than return to its 1957 price.

Fuel now represents a steadily increasing proportion of an airline's costs, however, and with every rise in fuel prices the amount of fuel an airliner burns becomes more important. Aircraft like the Boeing 747 are already operated well below their maximum design cruising speeds to save fuel. Steady rises in the cost of fuel seem inevitable. In the longer term, as industrial growth begins to outrun the world's petroleum resources, there will also be the effects of more costly exploitation of less accessible reserves of energy. Even if actual shortages of fuel may be some years off, rising fuel prices will become a fact of life. It may well prove worthwhile for the airlines to pay the research and development bill for new fuel-saving technology.

The twin problems of congestion and airport noise still exist. The year 1978 saw an amazing explosion in air travel within the United States and on the North Atlantic routes, traditionally the pacesetters for the rest of the world. Forced into cutting fares by government initiatives in the USA aimed at breaking the International Air Transport Association (IATA) control over international fares and bringing new blood into the US domestic industry, airlines found that with the right fare structures they could make money carrying passengers at far lower fare levels than ever before. Eight years after the wide-bodies entered service, the airlines finally found a way to pass the lower operating costs of the larger aircraft on to the travelling public.

In the medium term, it is almost certain that the twin pressures of traffic growth and airport congestion will be partly relieved by the introduction of stretched versions of existing types. In early 1979 McDonnell Douglas were offering stretched DC-10s seating 400 passengers for the US domestic airlines, and a 350-passenger aircraft with intercontinental range. Boeing's 747 has potential stretch in the fuselage, although it may prove hard to push the weight beyond the present 820,000 lb without major changes

to the wing. Airbus have studied a stretched version of the A300, and such aircraft will almost certainly appear in the 1980s.

The oldest of the current wide-body types is the 747. Some airlines are now flying 747s for more than 15 hours a day, at which rate there will be a substantial number of early 747s approaching 100,000 hrs by the end of the 1980s. It is accepted that aircraft structures cannot last indefinitely, while the cost of inspecting and regularly repairing the complex structure of an airliner can be crippling once the airframe starts to age. Given that some airlines will be looking for a 747 replacement in the 1990s, however, the next question must be: will it simply be another 747?

New technology may save enough fuel to pay the immense research and development bill for a new airliner, but a great deal of the new technology could be applied to derivatives of existing types. This is already being done in some cases; Pan American's new TriStar 500s are the first aircraft fitted with so-called "active ailerons", which use control surfaces to off-load the wing structure, permitting a longer-span wing without any great increase in airframe weight. The TriStar 500 wing is thus longer than that of the standard TriStar; longer, more slender wings produce less drag, particularly in the climb and cruise phases of flight.

New, more reliable and more capable electronic systems are now being introduced on some existing aircraft and their derivatives (such as the DC-9 Super 80). The new generation, such as the 767, will have even more advanced systems, in which cathode-ray tube displays will replace many of the conventional dials and counters. Such systems could, in fact, be introduced on existing aircraft.

The state of the art in wing design continues to advance. Active controls could be combined with drag-reducing wingtip winglets, producing significantly more efficient wings than the mid-1960s designs of the

Laker Airways' revolutionary Skytrain service sparked a revolution in low fares. Future aircraft will have to offer low costs to match

Appropriately symbolising the relative positions of the aircraft industry in the US and Europe, an Air Canada Boeing 747 towers over a BEA Trident 3B at London Heathrow. Runway congestion like this is becoming ever-present at all the major international airports and may force airlines to move to even bigger aircraft

747, TriStar and DC-10. Active controls, controlled by electronic systems to provide artificial stability, may allow versions of current airliners to be fitted with smaller tail surfaces, reducing drag still further; Lockheed may offer these systems on the TriStar from 1982.

It is possible, then, to foresee an airline replacing its existing 747 fleet in the early 1990s with some form of Advanced 747. Stretched by 50 ft, it might weigh nearly 1,000,000 lb in freighter configuration and could seat 700 passengers or more in a standard intercontinental layout. Active ailerons would allow 20 ft extensions to the tips of the existing wing, compensating for the greater weight. Powerplants would be developed from the present generation of engines, developing about 60,000 lb-thrust apiece; full-length engine cowls would keep the noise down to the same level as existing 747s, while being made largely of composite materials, such as graphite-epoxy, to offset the weight penalty of the larger cowling.

An all new aircraft, however, might burn significantly less fuel even than a 747 derivative. The wing of a new type could be much less sharply swept and hence lighter than that of the present 747s. The tail surfaces might be new and smaller, and the aircraft might rely entirely on electronics for its stability. The use of composites for "primary structure" – the main spars of the wing, for instance – promises massive weight gains, but the development of these composites for airline use will be a long and complex process. Two US military aircraft made their first flights in 1978 with wing and other sections of primary structure made of graphite-epoxy. However, the application of composites to airliners is likely to be complicated by the need to ensure equivalent safety to that enjoyed with conventional structures. New methods of testing and inspection will have to be devised, and tested themselves. Meanwhile, it is questionable whether the simple substitution of composites for conventional materials in existing aircraft will be worth the price, particularly when the composites have to compete with metal components which have been

The established types seem likely to remain in production for many years. A DC-10-30 is seen in Iberia's new livery, adopted in 1977

in production for a considerable period and are thus cheap.

Other items of new technology which might drive the airlines into acquiring completely new aircraft include the "prop-fan" being developed in the USA. This can either be regarded as an advanced propeller or an eight-bladed fan, using the latest, supercritical aerodynamics to produce a unit which may drive an aircraft at Mach 0.8 with 20 per cent more efficiency than a big-fan engine. Other concepts for "reducing energy powerplants" include Rolls-Royce's geared mid-fan engine, with the fan driven by epicyclic gearing and mounted half-way along the cowling.

Substantial fuel savings may be achieved if the industry can master the problems of laminar-flow control (LFC). Experiments with LFC have been carried out occasionally over the past 20 years or so, so far without producing a practical system. LFC operates by sucking air through a vast number of tiny perforations on the wing of the aircraft, stabilising the turbulence which is otherwise caused by friction between the air and the skin of the aircraft. Very large reductions in drag are possible if near-perfect laminar flow (that is, smoothly layered flow) can be achieved over the wings. The largest-scale use of LFC so far has been on the US National Aeronautics and Space Administration's Northrop X-21A, a 50,000 lb aircraft converted from a Douglas B-66 bomber and powered by two General Electric J79s. Two smaller engines were converted to draw air through the thousands of minute slots making up the LFC system. The tests with the X-21A showed up many of the snags associated with LFC, such as the high sensitivity of the system to the smallest foreign object or surface deformity. Nevertheless, LFC studies are continuing.

Will the subsonic passenger airliner be the only commercial type in service in the 1990s? In the USA, NASA and the main airframe manufacturers have carried out a considerable amount of work on the potential for a second-generation supersonic transport since the Boeing programme was cancelled in 1971. One company who have expended a great deal of effort on the SST pro-

gramme are McDonnell Douglas; their SST proposals have centred on the NASA "arrow-wing" configuration, a compound-sweep layout basically similar to a double-delta, but with a large slice taken out of the trailing-edge to reduce surface area and hence friction drag. Boeing, on the other hand, have looked at an SST with a fuselage blended smoothly into the wing. Lower noise levels than the first generation SSTs are a prerequisite, and this presents problems in the design of any new SST powerplant. Noise is a major limiting factor in the design of the McDonnell Douglas project, which would weigh 750,000 lb for take-off, almost as much as a 747. The engines could be variable-cycle powerplants, with internal valves enabling them to operate as turbofans for take-off and landing and turbojets in the cruise. These would, however, be

heavy and complex, as well as being extremely costly to develop. A more acceptable compromise may be a low-bypass-ratio turbofan proposed by Rolls-Royce, based on an Olympus core running at even higher pressure ratios than the Concorde powerplant. Unlike the similar low-bypass turbofans fitted to the Tupolev Tu-144, the proposed Olympus fan would be able to drive an SST at Mach 2 without reheat.

The McDonnell Douglas SST would seat up to 270 passengers (about as many as the abortive Boeing project), but would cruise in the same speed range – Mach 2.0–2.2 – as Concorde. The Boeing SST would have been faster, but the US manufacturers have apparently now decided that the extra speed is not worth the severe complications caused by structural heating. The range of the McDonnell Douglas

SST would be slightly greater than that of Concorde, allowing it to fly the longer over-water sectors which Concorde now has to fly with reduced payload.

However, any American SST would still have to avoid supersonic flight over land masses, and this would inevitably limit its market. It is also questionable whether its noise would be acceptable by the standards of the mid-1980s, using any foreseeable technology. Neither is it certain that its economics would stand comparison with the wide-bodies of today, let alone the stretched aircraft of the late 1980s; rising fuel prices would widen the economic gap between the classes of aircraft. Development costs would be astronomical, and the unit price could be shattering.

Another long-projected category of aircraft which could make its

In the 1980s, US freight airlines such as Seaboard will need a replacement for their McDonnell Douglas DC-8-63Fs, possibly a new specialised freighter

appearance in hardware form is the pure freighter. Rapidly advancing "deregulation" of the air freight market, particularly in the USA, may expand freight traffic to the point where the demand for a specialised freighter is large enough to justify its development. On the US domestic scene this trend may be helped by lower passenger fares, which have made cheap night flights less attractive to passengers. As the passenger airlines withdraw their night services, new opportunities open up for the freight carriers, as freight tends to travel overnight.

So far, the only commercial pure-freight aircraft to have sold in any numbers is the Lockheed L-100, basically a civil version of the Hercules military transport. Military cargoes tend to be denser than civil freight, so Lockheed have developed a series of stretched versions, culminating in the L-100-30, but they are planning an even further-stretched L-100-50, designed to replace DC-8s with the US freight airlines and nearly half as long again

as the original Hercules. The L-100-50 would be slower than the jets which it would replace, but fast enough for overnight deliveries anywhere in the USA; it would also burn less fuel and would be quieter. It would solve an increasingly pressing problem for some of the US freight airlines, which will not be allowed to operate their mainstay aircraft, the stretched DC-8, beyond 1985. But the question remains whether the market for a specialised freighter will ever be large enough to justify the development costs of an all-new aircraft. In the 1960s, Lockheed proposed developing civil freighters from their larger military jet freighters. The L-300, a stretched version of the C-141A StarLifter freighter, was actually ordered by two US airlines, but Lockheed decided not to go ahead with the project in the face of competition from the DC-8-63F. The L-500 would have been a commercial version of the C-5A Galaxy, the first of the jumbo jets, but no requirement existed for so vast an aircraft.

McDonnell Douglas proposed a

civil development of their YC-15 prototype, first flown in 1975 under a USAF contract to develop a replacement for the Hercules. The civil aircraft, designated Jet Trader 2, would be stretched to suit the lower density of civil freight, and would be fitted with four CFM56 turbofans.

Only in the Soviet Union has extensive use been made of pure-freight types in civil service. Aeroflot have operated Antonov An-12 freighters, basically similar to the An-10 airliner, but with a rear loading ramp like that of the Hercules. In the late 1960s, the Soviet airline introduced the massive Antonov An-22, at that time the largest aircraft in the world, on internal freight services. Aeroflot's involvement in freight operations is due to two factors. One has been the decision of the Soviet authorities to support mineral exploitation in Siberia by air rather than by land transport; the other is the airline's role as a military freighting reserve.

The An-22 was developed as a commercial and military strategic

freighter in the early 1960s. It has the same distinctively drooped wing as the An-12 and An-24, but is much larger, spanning 211 ft (16 ft more than a 747) and weighing 550,000 lb for take-off. It is powered by four of the massive Kuznetsov NK-12MV turboprops developed for the Tu-20 bomber and for its civil counterpart,

top
Outsize loads can be carried in aircraft like this Super Guppy, consisting of a vastly modified Boeing Stratocruiser airframe

above
Aeroflot use Antonov An-12s on Arctic support flights

243

McDonnell Douglas have proposed a specialised freighter based on the YC-15 military transport prototype. Known as Jet Trader 2, it would be considerably longer than this aircraft

the Tu-114, each delivering nearly 15,000 hp through eight-blade, contra-rotating propellers. About 100 An-22s were built between 1965 and 1974, and about half of these were delivered to Aeroflot. Landing on six pairs of massive low-pressure tyres, the big Antonovs have proved useful in the Tyumen oilfields, but they have not been extensively used outside the Soviet Union. The Antonovs have been seen abroad in airlift operations, and Aeroflot aircraft have been used to carry urgently needed military supplies to Russia's allies, but some aircraft have been lost on these flights.

Likely to enter Aeroflot service in rather greater numbers is the Ilyushin Il-76, also developed jointly for the air force and for the state airline. Flown in 1971, the Il-76 entered service with Aeroflot some four years later, initially on the oilfields. In 1977, Aeroflot took delivery of the first of the new Il-76T version, with slightly higher gross weight and increased fuel capacity, and deployed it on international scheduled freight services to Japan and Europe. The

Il-76 closely resembles the Lockheed StarLifter in layout, but is slightly larger. Slung under the wings are four 26,500 lb-thrust Soloviev D-30KP turbofans, uprated versions of the engine originally developed for the Il-62M; the long-range Il-76T can carry a 65,000 lb payload for 3,500 miles. The cabin volume is relatively small compared with the maximum payload, at least by Western commercial standards, indicating that the main role of the Il-76 is carrying heavy industrial or military equipment. Runway performance is respectable, due to triple-slotted trailing-edge flaps and full-span slats, and – like the An-22 – the jet freighter features a massive and heavy undercarriage for operations from unprepared airstrips. Like the StarLifter, the Il-76 has a high swept wing and a T-tail above the rear loading ramp, and the cabin is fitted with extensive cargo-handling equipment.

There is no doubt that aircraft such as the Il-76 or the projected L-300 have considerable advantages over converted airliners. Perhaps the

most important is that freight can be unloaded straight through massive rear doors onto a truck or cargo trailer, rather than being lowered item by item from the airliner's high door. The increased ease of loading translates directly into higher utilisation for the freighter, and more profit for the airline. However, the freight industry has not until now been sufficiently important to warrant development of a specialised aircraft. Despite this, the 1970s saw a number of advanced project studies aimed at meeting the need for a specialised freighter. Some of these were vast flying wings called "Spanloaders", in which freight would be carried within the wing section. By distributing the load along the wing, the structure could be made far more efficient and payload could rise to as much as half the gross weight of the aircraft. Some attention was also directed towards aircraft based on the Burnelli principle, in which the cargo would be carried in a broad, aerofoil-shaped fuselage. However, it is unlikely that such aircraft will make their appearance before more

modest developments such as the Jet Trader 2 and the L-100-50.

Another possible area of future development is the vertical take-off and landing (VTOL) or the short take-off and landing (STOL) commercial aircraft. The best established VTOL type, of course, is the helicopter, and it is possible to see a continuing and steadily expanding role for the type. British European Airways, Sabena and New York Airways were among the pioneers of

top
When this flew in 1968, it was the world's largest helicopter. With a rotor span of 115 ft and a fuselage length of 121 ft, the Mi-12 has twin decks and completely dwarfs the 31 ft-long Bell Jet Ranger in the foreground

above
British European Airways were pioneers of helicopter services, although the twin-rotor Bristol 173 of 1953 never went into service with the airline

The Lockheed C-5A Galaxy can swallow outsize loads, but the proposed L-500 commercial version was not proceeded with

commercial passenger-carrying helicopter services. Early helicopters used for these operations in the 1950s, such as the Sikorsky S-55, carried few passengers and were noisy (due to their powerful and heavy piston engines) and uneconomical. However, with the advent of the shaft-turbine engine and the first generation of large helicopters designed to use new, much lighter powerplants, the commercial heli-

copter became a practical proposition where the nature of the route demanded it. Foremost among the new generation of commercial helicopters was the 20-seater Sikorsky S-61, derived from the US Navy's SH-3 anti-submarine-warfare (ASW) helicopter. New York Airways built up a network of services linking central New York with the city's main airports (Kennedy, La-Guardia and Newark) with the S-61,

after pioneering the routes with the
twin-rotor Boeing 107. In the mid-
1960s, BEA started a less spectacular
but highly successful S-61 operation
linking the British mainland with the
Scilly Isles. (The helicopters replaced fixed-wing de Havilland
Herons.)

Vietnam was the helicopter's war,
and the requirements for increased
reliability and easier maintenance
which the US Army and Navy laid

down for their ASW and transport
helicopters after Vietnam led to
safer, more reliable and more economical helicopters for the airlines.
The development work which Boeing
put into the US Army's big, twin-
rotor CH-47 Chinook, first flown in
1960 as a big brother to the 107,
finally led in 1978 to an order from
British Airways for a 44-seat airliner
version, by a considerable margin the
largest practical helicopter produced

for airline use. Inescapable rotor
noise may limit the uses of helicopters
in city centres, but as new airports
are built at ever greater distances
from those city centres, VTOL may
be the only way to keep journey
times on short sectors within reason.

Noise, indeed, is one of the main
stumbling blocks to the development
of VTOL passenger vehicles faster
than the helicopter. One of the first
attempts to produce such an aircraft
was the British Fairey Rotodyne,
flown in 1958. The Rotodyne resembled a conventional twin-turboprop airliner with a high, stumpy
wing, but carried a single rotor on a
massive faired pylon above the fuselage. For take-off, the turboprops
pumped air to fuel burners on the
rotor tips, but the tip-jet-driven rotor
was unbelievably noisy and for this
and other reasons the programme
was abandoned. The same fate befell
the rather similar Russian Kamov
Ka-22.

Interest in VTOL/STOL for
everyday transport (as opposed to
the specialised applications, such as
inter-airport ferrying and oil-support

flights, for which helicopters are
used) revived in the early 1970s. The
British Government carried out extensive studies of VTOL airliners;
two design studies carried out about
that time were the Hawker Siddeley
HS.141, with a massive battery of
lift-fans located in sponsons on the
fuselage sides, and the Westland
WG.22, a vast tilt-rotor converti-
plane. The German Government
also showed considerable interest in
commercial VTOL, having sponsored development of the Dornier
Do31 experimental VTOL transport
in the mid-1960s. A German design
competition in 1970 yielded a
startling array of VTOL designs
including tilt-rotor, tilt-wing and
jet-lift types. Like the British designs,
all were intended to carry about 100
passengers. However, interest was
never strong on the airline side, and
the fad for VTOL projects ended
when it became obvious that such
aircraft would be immensely noisy,
even if they could be made to work
economically.

The USA worked on large VTOL
aircraft in the early 1960s, culmi-

above
An experimental STOL aircraft
is the Antonov An-2272, using the
Boeing-developed upper-surface-
blowing technique

opposite, top
The largest civil helicopter ordered
so far is the Boeing Commercial
Chinook, seating 44 passengers

opposite, bottom
After substantial expenditure of vast
sums of money and over four years
of exhaustive test flying, the Fairey
Rotodyne project was cancelled in
February 1962. BEA, the only
potential British operators,
concluded that the aircraft was not
a viable proposition

249

nating in the tilt-wing LTV XC-142A transport. Airline enthusiasm for VTOL was almost totally lacking, but the late 1960s saw an interesting Franco-US programme aimed at evaluating the practicality of operating a STOL aircraft on airline networks. The vehicle used was the French Breguet 941S, working on the deflected-slipstream principle; four Turbomeca Turmo turboprops drove big propellers which "washed" the entire short-span wing, which was fitted with powerful trailing-edge flaps. The attraction of the 941 was that it was basically a conventional aircraft, apart from the interconnecting spanwise linkage to ensure that all four propellers kept turning if one engine failed. Redesignated the McDonnell 188, the French STOL transport was extensively tested in the USA.

In 1970–72, the US airline industry showed considerable interest in a STOL aircraft that could offer reasonable economics while operating into city-centre "Stolports" barred to larger aircraft by noise and runway-length limitations. The de Havilland Canada Dash 7 was partly an answer to this general requirement, and may find an application in this rôle in the USA. In 1978, NASA flew a Quiet Short-Haul Research Aircraft (QSRA), converted by Boeing from a DHC C-8A Buffalo military freighter. The

QSRA is powered by four ALF 502 turbofans, mounted above and ahead of the wing and grouped well inboard. The engines exhaust over specially designed flaps which, when lowered, deflect the thrust downwards as water will follow the curved side of a wineglass. This system, known as upper-surface blowing (USB), was originally developed by Boeing for their YC-14 military freighter and permits extremely short take-off runs. USB aircraft are notably ugly, with their big engines flanking the flight-deck but they may become familiar in the 1990s.

One country with a continuing requirement for STOL aircraft is Japan, where the airline feeder system relies on many small Second World War 4,000 ft runways and local communities are resolutely opposed to the extension of existing strips. Japan's National Aerospace Laboratory plans to fly its own USB test-bed in 1982, based on a Kawasaki C-1 freighter and powered by four of Japan's own FJR-710 turbofans. The Japanese seem interested in developing their own STOL airliner for services from the late 1980s and, judging by their success in other branches of engineering, they could become a force to be reckoned with in the 1990s.

From time to time, there is a revival of interest in the airship as a freight- and passenger-carrying vehicle. In 1972, the British freight-shipping company, Manchester Liners studied a new technology rigid airship larger than the greatest of the Zeppelins, but nothing came of the proposal. Another British firm proposed a disc-shaped craft called the Skyship in 1977, claiming that such a craft would be easier to handle and more efficient than a conventional airship. However, it seems likely that the airship will remain confined to specialised tasks, such as aerial advertising; the romance of the great shadow in the clouds, and the almost-free lift gained from buoyancy, do little to offset the slow speed and consequently low productivity of even the most modern airship.

Hydrocarbon fuels are more difficult to replace in aviation than in any other application, so air transport may continue to exploit dwindling reserves while other industries turn to nuclear or solar energy. Eventually, however, the reserves may run dry, and air transport will have to look to alternative fuels. Atomic power was extensively studied by the US Air Force in the late 1950s, and requirement WS-125A for a nuclear-powered bomber with endurance measured in days rather than hours was formulated. A working reactor was test-flown in the NB-36H, a modified B-36 bomber equipped with a heavily shielded cockpit, but the aircraft was conventionally powered. Convair designed a massive canard test-bed, designated NX-2, but the nuclear-powered bomber was abandoned in favour of the chemically-fuelled B-70 Valkyrie. It is generally accepted that nuclear power for aircraft will have to await the development of the fusion reactor, harnessing the cleaner power of the longer-lasting thermo-nuclear reaction.

A great deal of effort has been put into the possible use of liquid hydrogen (LH) in aircraft. LH was used for the upper stages of spacecraft such as the Saturn rocket; its advantages are that it can be obtained by apply-ing energy to water, and that its supply thus depends only on the availability of ground-based sources of power. It is also immensely potent by unit of weight, the reason for its use in space launchers. However, it is not only far less dense than kerosene, but it only maintains its liquid state at very low temperatures; an LH-fuelled aircraft might thus have to carry enormous insulated fuel tanks almost as large as its fuselage. But if the fuel is so powerful, yet so hard to store, the answer may be to go higher and faster. Lockheed have proposed a vast LH-powered SST cruising at six times the speed of sound at altitudes well in excess of 100,000 ft, too high to leave a supersonic boom. It may seem to be a visionary dream, but even the giants of aviation history have often been proved too conservative in their predictions, and the madmen have often been proved right. Who could have foreseen the 747, even ten years before it flew? Many who saw the first, hesitant two-man flights have lived to see the wide-body jets; it is hard to say with any confidence that an industry which has accomplished such rapid progress has reached anywhere near the end of its achievements.

Japan's National Aerospace Laboratory plan to fly this STOL research aircraft in 1981, with a view to developing a STOL airliner

Index

top to bottom
DH 34, Vickers Vimy Commercial, Junkers F-13, *Graf Zeppelin*, Junkers G38.

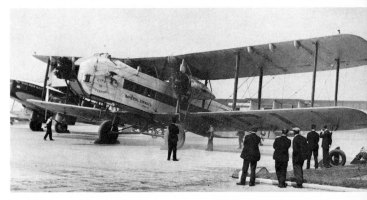

top to bottom
Farman Goliath, Le Bourget in 1933,
Armstrong Whitworth Argosy,
Junkers Ju 52, Short Scylla.

top to bottom
US Fokker F-10, Lockheed Electra,
Airspeed Ambassador, Douglas
DC-5, Vickers Viking.

right, top to bottom
Dornier DoX, Short Mayo composite,
Saunders-Roe Princess, Boeing 314
Clipper, Short Empire flying boat.

far right, top to bottom
Lockheed Super Electra, DH Comet
4C, Air France Caravelle, Tupolev
Tu-104, Boeing 727.